MEASURING SECURITY IN PERSONAL ADJUSTMENT

Mary D. Ainsworth and

Leonard H. Ainsworth

MEASURING

SECURITY

IN PERSONAL

ADJUSTMENT

UNIVERSITY OF TORONTO PRESS

FOREWORD

W. E. B L A T Z

Director, Institute of Child Study
University of Toronto

More than thirty years ago, a nursery school was started at the University of Toronto. From its early beginnings the main object of its organization was to provide an opportunity for studying the growth and development of children, chiefly from the psychological and social points of view. Furthermore, the emphasis was to be on the normal child.

Since then the Institute of Child Study has gradually evolved. In addition to research it has always conducted on parallel lines the application of research findings to the field of child training. Thus, side by side, the theoretical and the practical interests of the staff have been closely allied.

Out of this twofold task there gradually emerged a systematic outline of a way of understanding how children grow up and how human beings behave—even as adults.

Because discipline is the central theme of all child training, this aspect of the problem came under careful scrutiny. The role of the child was always to the forefront. It was inevitable, then, that the conscious state of the child should be the most significant aspect of the authority-child situation. And so the connection between a feeling of security and the appreciation of and attitude *towards* consequences was observed. The acquisition of new patterns of thinking and behaviour in this atmosphere of "consequences" through the mechanism of learning formed the basis of the dynamics of the theory.

Gradually the research studies carried on in the Institute began to centre around the concept of security, testing the theory but also evaluating the application of the theory in the field.

Among those who, in the early years, contributed to the combined efforts of the staff were the authors of this book. The first experimental study was published by one of them, Mary (Salter) Ainsworth, in

1940. Since then a goodly number of studies have been completed, of which many are cited in the following text.

In the first part of this book the authors have presented a concise outline of the theory of security as a descriptive doctrine of human development. Furthermore, they have illustrated how important is a knowledge of the normal to interpret the aberrant.

Then, they have shown how the theory lends itself to more precise scrutiny in the field. The detailed analysis which they have made and reported is a tribute to their skill and integrity. That the findings support the theory or not, is secondary to the fact that a method has been evolved to study the development of children in a social environment and, in addition, a scale of evaluation has been invented so that we may judge what kind of product the training plan produces.

This brings me to the chief reason for this preface, namely to congratulate the authors on a splendid piece of research in a complicated field.

PREFACE

The programme of test construction reported here is part of an extended research project directed by Dr. W. E. Blatz and guided by his theory of personality development, in which the concept of security has a focal position. The purpose of this extended investigation is to devise a series of tests that will measure the extent of a person's security and insecurity in a number of important areas in his life.

The four tests presented in this report have all been preceded by experimental versions. They are the outgrowth of a process of intimate interaction among theory, rationale and test construction. The first step in constructing each test was to devise a rationale that would guide the formulation of items. This rationale was drawn directly from Dr. Blatz's theory of development. Each successive attempt at test construction was evaluated in terms of how well it reflected the underlying rationale. Sometimes inadequacies in the rationale became apparent through the experience of test construction. In these instances it did not seem that the underlying theory was at fault, but rather that the rationale had been an inadequate representation of the theory. More frequently, the attempt at test construction seemed faulty because it did not reflect the rationale faithfully, and the next version of the test was planned to overcome these faults. Thus, throughout the programme, there was a constant process of checking back and forth between tests and rationale and between rationale and theory.

It will be impossible within the scope of this report to describe this process in detail. The main emphasis will be upon the present versions of the four tests and upon the rationale that guided their construction. Details of previous versions of the tests and their rationale will be given only in instances where they are pertinent to the construction of the present versions of the tests.

The present four tests cover only part of the total area of an individual's adjustment to life. The scope of the programme as a whole is considerably wider. Specifically, it is intended to develop tests of security and insecurity in each of the following important areas of adjustment:

(*a*) Familial intimacies: parent-child relations.

(*b*) Extra-familial intimacies: interpersonal relations outside the primary family. One very important aspect of interpersonal relations is that of heterosexual relations; for this special aspect a separate test seems desirable.

(*c*) Vocation: for the adult, adjustment to work; and for children, adolescents and young adults still in school, adjustment to academic work. Attitudes towards money constitute a special aspect of the vocational area and require a separate test.

(*d*) Avocations: leisure-time activities.

(*e*) Philosophy: religion or philosophy of life. There is a special aspect here, probably requiring a separate test: attitudes towards health, disease, accident and death.

The present set of tests deals with four of these five major areas, but not necessarily with the entire scope of each area. Specifically, we present here tests of security in the following aspects of adjustment: familial intimacies; extra-familial intimacies, excluding special reference to heterosexual relations; avocations; and philosophy of life, excluding special reference to health, disease, accident and death. These four aspects were selected because the rationale in each had been developed to a point at which a reasonably finished test could be expected to emerge, whereas the aspects omitted had been insufficiently explored.

These tests are intended for young adults of college age, but the test of familial security is the only one that is particularly limited to this age group. The programme as a whole embraces the range from early childhood to full maturity, with a set of tests appropriate to each important developmental level. Most of the work preceding this present study, and upon which it is based, was concerned with young adults of college age.

The first tests in this series were developed by one of us (M.D.A.) and reported in 1939 (10), and again, more briefly, in 1940 (11). There were two tests, covering the areas of familial and extra-familial intimacies. The programme was interrupted by the Second World War and not resumed until 1948–9, when Miss Mary Laurence (9) revised the familial test, adapting it to adolescents of high school age. Mrs. Marion Wright developed the first test of security in the philosophical area, while R. G. N. Laidlaw (8) and Dennis Roberts began work on tests relevant to the vocational area, Laidlaw dealing with adjustment of academic work and Roberts with attitudes towards money.* None of these tests, except that of Miss Laurence, was completed and reported in this phase.

During 1948–9 case histories were obtained by interviewing twenty student volunteers, to whom the Rorschach and Thematic Apperception Tests and all the tests of security developed by that time were also administered. The data were collected by a class of graduate students in a course in personality appraisal under the supervision of M.D.A. The analysis of data was undertaken in the summer of 1949 in the form of a series of clinical case studies, the purpose being to examine the degree of consistency between the findings of the security tests and clinical judgments based on the other data. These case studies were undertaken solely for the purpose of discovering weaknesses in the tests of security; they were neither written up nor submitted to statistical analysis. Together with the internal analysis of the tests themselves, these studies were invaluable in planning the next set of revisions.

During 1949–50 one of us (L.H.A.) produced the second revision of the familial test (1) suitable for young adults of college age. Mrs. Wright completed the first version of the philosophical test; it was administered to the same subjects as the familial test and its internal consistency was examined by L.H.A. (1). A first revision of the extra-familial test was developed in two parts to facilitate exploration of this area; B. W. Whitehouse (14) focused on the aspect of "belonging" and Miss O. J. Walter (13) dealt with the aspect of competition and status. Mrs. Mary Styffe constructed the first test of avocational security and Mr. Laidlaw (8) finished the first version of the vocational (academic) test which had been begun the year before. All of these tests were intended for people of college age. Further studies in the vocational area were undertaken at the same time. S. M. Tobin (12) constructed a test of security in the vocational adjustment of adults, and Miss M. H. Blum (3) developed one concerned with security in dealing with money, using high school students as her subjects. During the summer of 1950 the research team undertook further case studies and a more intensive statistical analysis of the tests that had been developed that year, including a check on the correlations between the various subtests.

In the next phase of the research, beginning in 1950–1, there were

*Mrs. Marion Wright, Mr. Dennis Roberts, and Mrs. Mary Styffe were members of the team which was investigating methods of assessing security in adjustment at the Institute of Child Study, University of Toronto.

several approaches, of which the present study is one. The only other study that will be mentioned here is M. F. Grapko's (6); Mr. Grapko, drawing upon the tests so far constructed, selected from them the best items, with or without some further revision, and pooled them into one test, which he called the ICS Scale (Institute of Child Study Scale). He used this scale as the basis for deriving a "mental health quotient." The present authors, on the other hand, retained the boundaries between the areas of adjustment and concentrated upon further refinements of the rationale in four areas in terms of the cumulative experience of the team; they developed four revised tests that might be used separately or in a battery. These were used first in a battery, because this phase of test construction was a preliminary step to another study (2) in which a generalized measure of insecurity was required.

In the report which follows we shall offer, first, a very brief account of the theory that gave rise to the whole project and upon which the rationale of the tests was based. It is inappropriate here to present the theory in detail, but it would be inconvenient to attempt to present the rationale of the tests without having first introduced a few essential concepts. Secondly, we shall give an account of the methods used in constructing the revised tests, describing their basic structure, the formulation of items, the instructions, and the methods used to check the validity of the items in terms of internal consistency. Thirdly, we shall deal with each test in turn, first giving the rationale that guided the selection of items, and then considering the results of the item analysis. Finally, the reliability of the tests will be discussed and the results of intra-test and inter-test comparisons will be presented.

M. D. A.
L. H. A.

ACKNOWLEDGMENTS

First, we are happy to acknowledge the debt we owe to Dr. W. E. Blatz, whose theory of the focal role in human development played by the search for security was the starting point of the research programme from which stemmed the work reported here. His stimulation and encouragement not only made this book possible, but also has been a significant force in our own lives over a period of many years.

We wish also to express our gratitude to the members of the research team at the Institute of Child Study, University of Toronto, who like ourselves have been concerned with understanding and measuring the ways in which people seek to achieve security in their personal adjustment. Those members of the team whose work has laid the foundation for ours have been mentioned in the introduction to this book, and more detailed acknowledgment is interspersed throughout the text of the book itself. The list would not be complete without mention of others who have been helpful and interested. We wish to extend thanks to Dr. Mary L. Northway, both for her active help in the arrangements for publication and for her interest and encouragement throughout the study. Thanks also to Professor Dorothy Millichamp and Mrs. Betty Flint for their interest, and for the valuable contributions they are making in parallel research into the early years of development.

To Dr. R. W. B. Jackson and his staff in the Department of Educational Research, Ontario College of Education, we extend our thanks for advice and help in the statistical treatment of our findings.

We very much appreciate the help given us by the staff members of the Medical School of University College, and the Psychology Departments of University College, Bedford College, Birkbeck College and the School of Economics of the University of London in making subjects available to us. We wish to thank also the students in these colleges who contributed their time in response to our requests.

Finally, we wish to express our gratitude to the Defence Research Board of Canada. The Security Studies reported in this book were supported in part by the Research Board, under Grant Number 58. We trust that their faith in the value of basic research will be justified in ample measure.

CONTENTS

MEASURING SECURITY IN PERSONAL ADJUSTMENT

I A BRIEF STATEMENT OF THEORY

Insecurity is experienced by the individual when he is unable to satisfy his needs or anticipates being unable to do so. It is a common component of such feelings as distress, anxiety, grief, frustration, conflict, and pain. Insecurity occurs when the person is prevented from satisfying primary and secondary needs alike, but it does not always arise as a result of a state of need, for when the person experiences a need, whether it be hunger or a desire to spend a pleasant evening in congenial company, he is not insecure if he anticipates that his need will be satisfied in due course. Only when the need is so acute that it brooks no delay, or when the person can anticipate no satisfaction, is there full insecurity.

According to this definition, insecurity is a motivating state since the individual who experiences insecurity has a need to reduce or terminate it. Various possibilities are open to him. He may learn a new pattern of behaviour which solves the problem implicit in the situation, and by that means he reduces insecurity by eliminating its cause. This is the "independent" solution. Or he may appeal to other persons to act on his behalf and deal with the situation that produces his insecurity. This is the "dependent" solution. Or he may utilize any one of a variety of defence mechanisms to reduce the insecurity which he subjectively experiences without doing anything to change the situation which aroused the insecurity in the first place. This is referred to by Dr. Blatz as the solution through "deputy agents."

It is now commonly accepted among students of child development that insecurity (or anxiety) is the primary state of the infant. His needs are felt acutely and yet he lacks adequate means to satisfy them himself; if they are not immediately satisfied he is overwhelmed by his discomfort, since he has no basis for anticipating that this state of affairs will not continue indefinitely. It is only gradually that he comes to depend upon his parents, especially his mother, as agents. To the extent to which they are skilful in interpreting, and, indeed, anticipating his needs and satisfying them, the infant is enabled to attain a state of dependent security. The infant *is* in fact dependent upon his parents or parent substitutes from the beginning, but it takes him some time to *feel* dependent, to recognize the parent as the agent for satisfying his needs, and it takes perhaps even longer for him to feel secure in this dependence, to trust that this agent will be promptly effective. Once a basis of dependent security is built up, the child handles insecurity in the obvious way—by calling the parent to his assistance. This is the "immature dependent" solution.

In the normally healthy course of development the child gradually learns to depend less and less upon his parents as agents for satisfying his needs and reducing his insecurity, and to depend more and more upon himself. There are probably two chief contributing factors here. First, the parents, of necessity, fall short of omnipotence and omniscience. They are unable to interpret and anticipate all the child's needs, and they cannot shield him from all insecurity. But to the extent to which they provide a generally secure background, the infant or young child becomes able to tolerate some degree of insecurity without falling back always on the "dependent" solution. Given a generally secure basis from which to work, the young child gradually learns skills through which he can independently gain satisfactions. Secondly, the very process of maturation of motor and perceptual capacities brings its own basis for the development of independence, for the child gains satisfactions through the exercise of these capacities and becomes increasingly independent of parental efforts on his behalf. First in connection with small frustrations, and gradually even in critically insecure situations, the growing child turns more and more readily to the "independent" way of handling insecurity.

This gradual shift from dependent to independent solutions takes place at different rates of speed and to differing degrees of completeness. Up to a certain point, the more insecure the child, the more likely he is to cling to the familiar instead of risking increased insecurity by venturing into new situations that will help him to learn new skills. Although his state of dependence is more insecure than secure, he clings to it.

Even in instances where the continuing dependence is predominantly secure it is potentially much more insecure than an equivalent degree of security resting largely upon independence. As the child grows up, his parents find it increasingly difficult to act as his agents, and often become increasingly less disposed to do so. To the extent to which his parents cannot or do not continue to take responsibility for him, the child is thrown into insecurity which is all the more difficult to handle since he has failed to build up the skills and experience necessary for the adoption of the independent solution towards which he is being forced.

From the prognostic point of view, the independent solution is much more satisfactory than continuing reliance upon the parents. The independently secure person has built up confidence in himself as his own agent through the acquisition of skills. His past experience not only gives him a feeling of security in handling situations which previously aroused insecurity, but also gives him confidence that he can learn to handle new situations. He has faith in himself and in his ability to learn. Thus, the independent solution brings with it a large measure of tolerance for insecurity, because the initial experience of insecurity in a new situation is less acute if the person can anticipate that he will be able to overcome it.

Nevertheless, the effectiveness of the independent solution is limited. To a large extent even the most competent adults must rely upon other people to assist them in satisfying their needs and protecting them against insecurity generally. The mutual dependence characteristic of the co-operative relationships used by mature adults to overcome the limitations of the independent solution must, of course, be distinguished from the dependence of young children. Whereas young children are essentially recipient in their dependency, mature adults are mutually contributing in theirs. The young child must rely upon dependency because he lacks skills, but both or all parties to a co-operative endeavour must contribute their separate competencies if a successful state of interdependence is to be attained. It is equally important that each of those concerned should be able to maintain a relationship in which he is aware of the insecurities of the others, able to interpret and to some extent anticipate their needs, and motivated to act as an agent for the satisfaction of those needs. To the extent to which the person's security rests upon mutually contributing relationships of this kind he has "mature dependent security." To the extent to which his security rests upon other people in the essentially recipient and non-contributing way characteristic of the young child, he has "immature dependent security."

All these methods of seeking and achieving security have one thing in common—they reduce insecurity by dealing with its cause. This is so whether the person acts on his own behalf or whether he depends on other people to serve as his agents. There is a fourth method, involving defence mechanisms, by means of which the person may rid himself of the feelings that constitute insecurity, but neither satisfy the need involved nor change the situation that aroused these feelings in the first place. This solution is through deputy agents. Whereas other agents (including the self as agent) are constructive, these deputy agents play a purely analgesic role. As such, they perform a useful function for those in intolerably insecure situations where no other agents are readily available. Sometimes they can be used in conjunction with other agents. Since acute insecurity interferes with learning and thus makes the independent solution a difficult one to adopt, the reduction of insecurity through defence mechanisms may make it possible for the individual to proceed towards a more constructive solution.

It is, however, more likely that the analgesic mechanism will, through its very role of reducer of insecurity, prevent the person from seeking a more satisfactory solution. In this case, the unsatisfied need that gave rise to the original insecurity may well grow stronger with continued frustration and insecurity will recur. If insecurity is again to be staved off, the defences must be redoubled. Even though the need subsides, and the defences may be relaxed, the "deputy agent" solution shares with the "immature dependent" solution the disadvantage that the person is no more capable of handling the insecure situation when it recurs than he was before. There is a further disadvantage in that the defence mechanism itself may be of such a nature as to create further difficulties for the individual and thus give rise to further insecurity. It is a common clinical observation that defence mechanisms tend to lead into a vicious spiral in which ever-increasing anxiety causes ever-increasing defences, which in themselves create more difficulties, until, finally, the person is entirely absorbed in a purely defensive operation and has little energy left for anything else.

II METHODOLOGY

The Structure of the Tests

The purpose of the tests is not only to assess the extent to which an individual is secure or insecure, but also to describe the methods whereby he attempts to attain or maintain security. To accomplish this purpose, five subtests are required, one for each of independent security, mature dependent security, immature dependent security, insecurity, and deputy agents. In certain areas of adjustment not all of the four methods for overcoming insecurity are theoretically possible; in such instances the test includes only those subtests that deal with the possible methods. Two such areas of adjustment are the familial and philosophical areas, for reasons that will be presented when the rationales for the tests in these areas are discussed. Therefore, the familial and philosophical tests have only four subtests each, whereas the extra-familial and avocational tests follow the basic structure requiring five subtests.

This basic structure has been followed, with necessary modifications, in constructing all the tests since the first two were developed (10, 11). These two early versions measured a single continuum of security-insecurity, but even in them there was some attempt to describe the means whereby the person attempted to attain or maintain security. Thus, the first familial test was provided with a supplementary scale of independence-dependence, and the first extra-familial test had a supplementary scale of tolerance-intolerance which was intended to take account of one type of defence mechanism used to reinforce security.

The previous versions of the tests were experimental, designed to explore the area, and they were considerably longer than the present tests. It was intended that the present battery of four tests should be brief enough to be administered in one classroom hour. With this in mind, it was planned that the independent security, mature dependent security and immature dependent security subtests should contain six items each, and that the deputy agents and insecurity subtests should have twelve items. The extra-familial and avocational tests therefore contain forty-two items each, and the familial and philosophical tests, which have only four subtests, contain thirty-six items each.

Formulation of Items

All items are phrased in the form of a statement rather than a question, and the subject is required to indicate those statements which he feels to be applicable to himself and his own feelings. Since security is a subjective state, it is more appropriate that the subject be asked to deal with statements describing feelings than statements describing or evaluating behaviour. Throughout the programme some effort was made to formulate items in subjective terms, but the subjective formulation is different enough from the accustomed phrasing of items of tests and questionnaires to be difficult, and hence the early versions of the tests were not consistently subjective. In the course of experience with the tests, the conviction grew that it was essential for each item to describe a subjective state, and in the present tests this principle was followed consistently in formulating the items. We attempted to avoid one trap into which we and other team members had fallen previously, namely, the assumption that the words "I feel" prefixed to a statement would give the item a subjective formulation. This assumption is, of course, unfounded. In formulating the items of the present tests we attempted to go further than this and have each item reflect either a positive (secure) or a negative (insecure) feeling.

This was not possible with the items of the deputy agents subtests, which present a special problem with respect to subjective wording. In these subtests the emphasis is on the presence or absence of a mode of adjustment rather than upon subjective experience. Consequently, the individual does not report primarily upon feelings of ease, comfort and confidence or their converse, but rather upon specific attitudes or patterns of behaviour. Nevertheless, an attempt was made to frame the deputy agents items so as to invite a subjective report, since it is believed that a person can more validly report how he feels than evaluate himself objectively or predict his behaviour in a hypothetical situation. In this case the subjective report does not, of course, reflect directly feelings of security or insecurity. If the person endorses both a significant number of these items and a significant number of items reflecting security, the assumption is that his defence mechanisms are working successfully to prevent insecurity; but if he endorses a significant number of items in the insecurity subtests, it is assumed that the defence mechanisms are failing in their function of protecting against insecurity.

The deputy agents subtests demand even more co-operation from the subject than the other subtests, and a certain degree of insight as well. Therefore, an absence of endorsements within the deputy agents subtest cannot be taken to mean that the individual does not use defence mechanisms. It may simply mean that he is quite unaware of using them. This difficulty cannot be overcome entirely even with subjects who fall within the normal range of adjustment. However, an attempt was made to minimize the difficulty by framing the items of the deputy agents subtest in a way that would least challenge the defences of the subject, that is, by avoiding statements that he would dislike to acknowledge about himself even though he knew they were true.

We have deliberately abandoned an attempt to avoid double-barrelled statements. In the first tests this avoidance was a criterion for framing items, in accordance with the usual practice in constructing questionnaires and pencil-and-paper tests. But the more refined the rationale became, the more desirable it seemed to frame items that subsumed the various points by which one kind of adjustment might be distinguished from another. This will be illustrated with reference to the independent security subtests of the familial test where the items must reflect security as well as independence, and must be double-barrelled in order to do so. We are not aware that the inclusion of such constructions has made difficulties for the subject in replying.

Instructions

The subject is instructed to read each statement carefully and to indicate whether he feels that the statement is applicable to him at the present time. He is told to indicate "true" if he feels the statement applies to him, "false" if he feels it does not apply, and "cannot say" or "?" if he is undecided. These instructions are printed at the top of the first test of the battery, the familial test, and the four tests follow in order, distinguished only by the headings: Part I, Part II, Part III, and Part IV. In administering the tests to the sample population, the examiner read the instructions aloud to the groups of subjects.

Subjects

The subjects were 175 first- and second-year students at the University of London. They included students of medicine, sociology, social science, economics, and psychology. There were ninety-five men and eighty women. The ages ranged from eighteen to forty-five, but only twenty were over twenty-four years of age.

Scoring

Each subtest was scored simply by assigning a score of one to each "true" answer, assuming that the items were of equal weight; the item scores were then summed to obtain the subtest score. For the purposes of most of our analysis only the "true" answers were considered, but later there was some attempt to analyse the distribution of "cannot say" answers and to utilize them. This will be discussed below in the report.

Item Analysis

Throughout the construction of the tests there have been two chief criteria of the usefulness of an item: (a) the frequency with which it was endorsed as "true" by the sample population, and (b) the extent to which it was consistent with the subtest in question. An item was considered unsatisfactory if a "true" answer was given by more than 79 per cent or fewer than 10 per cent of the sample. The criterion of internal consistency used was the correlation coefficient devised by Ferguson (5); this is a highly exacting criterion. It provides for a measure of the extent to which the item in question distributes the sample as it is distributed by the subtest as a whole. A coefficient of .20 is considered satisfactory in the experimental stages of developing a test, but .30 is required before an item may be included in the final test. The latter criterion was the one used in this study.

Reliability

The criterion of reliability used in the present study was Hoyt's coefficient (7) derived from an analysis of variance, which is, in effect, based also upon a criterion of internal consistency. Reliability coefficients were found for each subtest separately, and for the pooled scores of each type of subtest in the test battery as a whole.

Inter-correlations among Subtests

A subtest, internally consistent and reliable, may yet not measure what it is intended to measure, and so lack validity. To us the most obvious first step in checking the validity of a subtest was to refer to the rationale which defined what the subtest was supposed to measure. According to the rationale, certain relationships between this subtest and other subtests could be specified as required, and a check could be made to ascertain whether these specifications were met. For example, there should be a significant negative correlation between the subtest designed to measure independent security in a given area of adjustment and the subtest designed to measure insecurity in the same area. Moreover, there should be a positive relationship between an independent security subtest and the corresponding mature dependent security subtest. The same trends should be apparent when comparing the independent security subtest with mature dependent security and insecurity subtests in other tests, but the relationships would not be expected to be as close as those found within the same test. These expectations from the rationale will be given in more detail after the rationale itself has been presented.

It is an obvious short-coming of the present study that the only criteria of validity used are internal ones, but they were the only ones feasible within its scope. When one considers that security is, by definition, subjective and that the tests are complex ones in which each subtest would probably require separate outside criteria, it is obvious that it is a considerable task to validate adequately a battery consisting of eighteen subtests. It seemed only reasonable to subject the battery of tests to an exacting internal test first, and only if it met this test adequately, to recommend more extensive studies of validity.

III SECURITY IN FAMILIAL INTIMACIES

Throughout the first three versions of the familial test considerable difficulty was encountered with the subtests designed to measure independent security and immature dependent security. It is, therefore, proposed to give a brief account of the earlier versions of the test, with particular reference to the development of these two subtests, before presenting the rationale that guided the construction of the present version of the test—the third revision. A discussion of the subtests of insecurity and deputy agents, including the contributions made by the first three versions of the test, will be deferred until the rationale of these subtests in the third revision is presented.

The First Familial Test

The first familial test (10, 11) consisted of two scales, one measuring security-insecurity and the other measuring independence-dependence. Although the items reflecting security did not allow a distinction to be made between independent and dependent security, this distinction was provided by the supplementary scale of independence-dependence.

The original list of 140 items covered those aspects of parent-child relations believed by clinicians to reflect the satisfactory or unsatisfactory nature of the adjustment of the young adult to his family. A few of the items were phrased subjectively and gave a direct report of security or insecurity. Most of the items dealt either with behaviour patterns from which security or insecurity might be inferred, or with conditions, such as attitudes of parents, believed to affect the degree of security experienced. The superiority of the subjectively worded item was not fully realized until the scales were finalized, and the failure to have framed all the items thus was believed to be a serious weakness of this first test.

Relatively few of the original items were retained in the final scale, most of them failing to meet a criterion of internal consistency in the course of administration to successive samples of university students. The final test included only forty-two items unevenly distributed among the four sections of the test.

The independence-dependence scale was intended to indicate the degree to which the individual felt emancipated from control by his parents and from the need for their emotional support. An examination of the items that met the criterion of internal consistency suggests that this intention was fulfilled. It is the security section of the test which is the least satisfactory. Only seven items remained in this section after the inconsistent items were pulled out, and these reflected little more than the absence of friction between the young person and his parents. The test thus described the independently secure person as one who has emancipated himself from his parents and who experiences little or no friction in his current relations with them; it did not add to this description, as the basic theory requires, that he is one who has confidence in himself and in his own skills as a basis for managing his own affairs. The test described the dependently secure person as one who is dependent on his parents and who experiences no disharmony with them over the issue of emancipation; it did not add to the description that he is one who has a sound basis of trust and confidence in his parents.

The First Revision of the Familial Test

In the first revision of the familial test the major task was to change the focus of attention from emancipation as such to the underlying faith and confidence in the parents which constitutes the basis for dependent security and to the confidence in self and skills which is the necessary condition for the transition from dependent to independent security. To implement this change in emphasis, Laurence (9) abandoned the separate scale of independence-dependence, and substituted subtests dealing with independent security and dependent security. The latter was not specified as immature dependent security, but this was implicit in Laurence's rationale. A third subtest dealt with insecurity, and a fourth with deputy agents, the latter having been omitted in the first test. The test was intended for high school students rather than college students, in the belief that dependent security might be explored more effectively with the younger subjects.

As described by the items of the test, the independently secure adolescent is one who has confidence in his own ability to meet situations by himself; he feels that he is free from domination by his parents, that he plays a participant adult role in family life, and that there is mutual trust and confidence in his relations with his parents. The dependently secure adolescent is one who feels warmth and a sense of belonging in the family group, and who is satisfied with a continuing state of dependence on the parents with respect to a variety of specific issues.

When the test was administered to a group of 141 high school students it was found that the items in both the independent security and the dependent security subtests were endorsed too frequently for them to be differentiating. Moreover, a very high positive correlation was found between the scores on the two subtests—a finding that is contrary to the requirements of the rationale, since the very independence achieved by the independently secure person should make it impossible for him to endorse items reflecting the continuing dependence implicit in dependent security. Case studies subsequently confirmed the statistical findings. Some of the best-adjusted subjects, who by all clinical criteria had achieved independent security, were classed as dependently secure by the Laurence test. On the other hand, it was found that items intended to reflect independent security could be endorsed by subjects who, while conforming to parental demands that pushed them towards adult responsibilities, might be described as feeling a need to conform and a longing to regress to childish dependence so marked as to require them to be classed as highly dependent.

The Second Revision of the Familial Test

The theory formulated by Dr. Blatz excluded the possibility of mature dependent security in the relationship between an individual and his parents. He held that the primary tie was of such a nature that continuing dependence necessarily retained a quality of immaturity, and that the only mature and secure adjustment came about through the person's acquiring enough independent security to be able to sever the primary tie, thus becoming free to continue his development through both independence and the establishment of interdependent relations with others outside the family. Retention of the tie with the parents was held to interfere inevitably with this development.

The difficulties encountered in the first revision of the test led us to question this formulation and to propose that in the residual warmth and sense of belonging characteristic of the well-adjusted young adult in his relations with his parents there is a quality akin to mature dependent security, that this quality was not incompatible with independent security, and that it could be distinguished from the regressive clinging to parental support which is believed to be characteristic of immature dependent security. On this basis one of us (L.H.A.) (1)

prepared a second revision of the test including a mature dependent security subtest, as well as subtests covering independent security, immature dependent security, insecurity, and deputy agents.

As defined by those items that met the criterion of internal consistency, the independently secure person is one who has confidence in his ability to make his own way without help from his parents, who is emancipated from parental control, demands and expectations, and who, at the same time, has comfortable relations with his parents. This definition seemed closely in line with the underlying rationale. The mature dependently secure person was defined as one who feels warmth and affection for his parents but who is distinguished from the immature dependently secure person by the fact that his warm relations with his parents, although valued, were not relied upon as a major source of emotional support. Thus, the independent security subtest stressed a secure emancipation and the mature dependent security subtest stressed continuing warm relations with parents, but both subtests included both components. The overlap was so great that a very high positive correlation was found between the two subtests, suggesting that both were measuring the same thing and that an adequate distinction between independent and mature dependent security had not been made.

The second revision of the immature dependent security subtest attempted to make the distinction between independent and immature dependent security more clear-cut than it had been in the first revision. The items emphasized dependence on the parents to fulfil needs—especially needs for affection and approval—and to take responsibility for decisions. The dependence was described as being maintained by accepting parental demands, discipline and control.

Although it had been intended to stress security as well as dependence, the inter-correlations among the subtests demonstrated that this stress had been insufficient. Four of the items were related positively to the insecurity subtest, and the subtest as a whole had a substantial positive relationship with the deputy agents subtest. Case studies confirmed the impression that some of the items that had been intended to reflect immature dependent security were endorsed by subjects who, by other criteria, were markedly insecure in relations with their parents.

The Third Revision of the Familial Test

Experience with the second revision of the familial test led to the conclusion that there was no justification for including a mature de-

pendent security subtest in the familial test. The third revision therefore consists of four subtests, namely, independent security, immature
dependent security, deputy agents and insecurity. The test may be seen
in the Appendix, where the items are grouped according to subtest for
convenience of reference although the items from all subtests were
pooled at random when presented to the sample population. Each
subtest will be considered separately in the ensuing discussion.

Independent Security

The chief conclusion that stemmed from our work with previous
versions of the test was that the independent security subtest should
give equal emphasis to the emancipated self-confidence that had been
stressed in the independent security subtest of the second revision and
to the good relations with the parents that had been stressed in the
mature dependent security subtest of that revision. To ensure that this
dual emphasis was indeed present, *every* item of the independent
security subtest of the third revision was designed to reflect both of
these aspects. The items thus define the independently secure person
as one who has confidence in his own competence to make his own
way, who is emancipated from dependence on parental support, help,
control and affection, and who has continuing satisfactory relations with
his parents. The items for the subtest were drawn from both the
independent and the mature dependent security subtests of the second
revision, the criterion being that the item should have a high coefficient
of internal consistency with the independent security subtest of that
revision. Three items were taken over unchanged and three other items
were revised in order to give adequate stress to both of the components
considered essential in the definition of independent security.

Immature Dependent Security

The chief task in revising the immature dependent security subtest
was to frame the items in such a way that they emphasized security
as well as dependence, since the chief defect of this subtest in the
second revision was that it was too closely related to the subtests
measuring insecurity and deputy agents. The task was a difficult one,
because dependence on parents is so frequently a manifestation of
insecurity when it occurs with young adults that one might well ask
whether it is possible for a young adult to be both dependent on his
parents and secure in this relationship. It is believed that this is pos-

sible, but that whenever it occurs it has implications of retarded development in interpersonal relations, or regression. It might occur if the person as a child was handicapped in developing both skills and friendships, while still having good relations with his parents, so that he has continued to cling to them for lack of an adequate basis for security elsewhere. Or perhaps what was once a secure child-parent relationship has at one time been badly shaken, and has only gradually been re-established, and this process has taken precedence over the process of emancipation. Or perhaps the parents have tied their child to them so skilfully that the happiness he experiences in the state of dependency is marked enough to obscure the feelings of frustration arising from interference with the process of emancipation.

In the present revision, each item of the immature dependent security subtest has two components, one specifying a state of dependence and the other specifying that this state is deeply satisfying to the person. The immature dependently secure person is defined by these items as one who relies upon his parents for help, advice and affection, and who finds satisfaction in so doing and in the close, warm relations existing between him and his parents. All of the items in this subtest were derived from the second revision, but all but one had to be revised to ensure that the desired dual emphasis was included.

Insecurity

The insecurity subtests of all versions of the familial test deal only with insecurity as it is experienced by persons who have had enough support from their parents to permit the development of immature dependent security to some extent, and consequently to permit the development of a capacity for interpersonal relations and distress when these relations go awry. Clinical experience suggests that if primary insecurity continues—that is, if the young child is unable to count on his parents or parent surrogates for the basic support, both material and emotional, that he needs for his development—a very disturbed and highly defensive pattern of adjustment ensues. One of the results of this extremely disturbed adjustment is that the person, even as an adult, is so handicapped in his communication with others and in insight into his own needs and feelings that pencil-and-paper tests cannot reflect the nature and extent of his maladjustment.

The insecurity section of the first familial test (10, 11) contained twenty-one items that met the criterion of internal consistency. Over half of these dealt with the insecurity implicit in the friction a young adult has in relations with his parents when he feels that they are interfering with his efforts to choose his own friends and manage his own affairs. Most of the remaining items dealt with conditions in the family that might be assumed to occasion insecurity but not with actual insecurity itself.

In the first revision, Laurence (9) still placed the major emphasis on friction over the issue of emancipation, but also included items intended to reflect a more fundamental insecurity consisting of feelings of being neglected or rejected by the parents.

In the second revision (1), an attempt was made to broaden further the coverage of the insecurity subtest. In addition to items reflecting friction over the emancipation process three classes of items proved satisfactory according to the criterion of internal consistency: (a) items involving irritation with the parents over matters not related to emancipation; (b) items reflecting insecurity related to the dependent state itself—those concerned with over-sensitivity to parents' disapproval, distress because of inability to live up to parents' expectations, and so on and (c) items simply describing unhappy parent-child relations.

Thus constituted, the insecurity subtest proved satisfactory in internal consistency and in meeting the expectations of the rationale in its relationships with other subtests. But the items on the whole were too infrequently endorsed, and this suggested that they reflected a degree of insecurity too extreme to be experienced by any but a very few in this population.

In constructing the third revision of this subtest some of the items that had been infrequently endorsed were dropped and others were reworded with the intention of making them less extreme. New items were added which were intended to reflect the insecurity felt by the person so lacking in self-confidence that he is apprehensive about the attenuation or end of support from his parents that the future will inevitably bring.

To summarize, the insecurity subtest contains four main classes of items: (a) items reflecting unhappy relations with the parents, with the nature of the difficulty unspecified; (b) items reflecting friction between the subject and his parents that is directly or indirectly related to his efforts to emancipate himself from them; (c) items reflecting an insecure state of dependence, characterized by oversensitivity to parents' disapproval and fear of failure in meeting their expectations; (d) items reflecting fear of loss of dependence and lack of self-confidence with respect to emancipation.

Deputy Agents

Difficulties experienced by the very young child in his relations with his parents are believed by most clinicians to have an all-pervasive influence upon his adjustment in other areas of life both in childhood and afterwards. Furthermore, it is believed that the defence mechanisms established by the child in an attempt to handle insecurity in his relations with his parents tend to be carried over into his relations with other people and to be perpetuated in adult life. When dealing with the adult it is very difficult, if not impossible, to distinguish between those defence mechanisms with their origins in parent-child relations and those with later origins in other areas of adjustment. This constitutes a problem in constructing a subtest to measure the extent to which the adult makes use of defence mechanisms in his intimate relations with his parents. Should such a subtest include all mechanisms believed to have their origin in parent-child relations? Or should it confine itself to mechanisms manifesting themselves in current parent-child relations?

The decision made at the time of the third revision of the familial test, and implicit in earlier revisions, was to include mechanisms that manifest themselves in current parent-child relations and mechanisms that are so generalized as to run through all areas of adjustment, but to exclude those that manifest themselves chiefly in the areas dealt with specifically by other tests in this series.

The first revision of the familial test (9) was the first to include a subtest dealing with defence mechanisms or deputy agents. Two mechanisms only were included in the items which met the criterion of internal consistency. One of these, over-conformity to parents' standards, has been retained in all subsequent revisions. This mechanism is believed to arise because the child does not feel sure of his parents' affection and attempts to avoid disapproval and to win affection by a rigid conformity to what he believes his parents expect of him. The other mechanism—getting one's own way with parents by sulking or coaxing—was not retained in subsequent revisions because it seemed inappropriate to the somewhat higher age level for which the test was intended.

In the second revision (1), two mechanisms in addition to over-conformity were represented in the items that met the criterion of internal consistency. The first was procrastination, which is believed to arise as a defence against the insecurity occasioned by pressure towards an unwelcome independence—making decisions and taking responsibility for actions—when the young person would prefer that his parents continue as his agents in these matters. The second mechanism was rebellion against authority, which is believed to arise from insecurity associated with an inability to achieve a desired independence of parents. Those who achieve emancipation without independent security may carry over resentment from parents to figures of authority in general.

These three mechanisms together—over-conformity, procrastination and rebellion against authority—formed a subtest that met the requirements of the rationale in two important ways. It proved first to be negatively related to the independent security subtest of the familial test; this was expected since the person whose security rests upon confidence in himself and his own competence, and who is emancipated from his parents on this basis, should not need to use defence mechanisms in his relations with his parents. Secondly, there was a low positive correlation with the insecurity subtest of the familial test; this was expected because defence mechanisms tend not to be a satisfactory protection against the insecurity they are established to counteract. On the other hand, there was a significant positive relationship with the immature dependent security subtest; this was not expected since any subtest reflecting security should not be significantly related in a positive direction to a subtest measuring defence mechanisms. This relationship may be explained by the fact that two of the defence mechanisms in the subtest—over-conformity and procrastination—represent a clinging to the "dependent solution," a solution that is also reflected by the immature dependent security subtest. Moreover, the latter subtest in the second revision over-emphasized dependence and under-emphasized security, and because of this the entire subtest could be viewed as reflecting dependence as a defence mechanism and as representing an attempt to achieve security but not necessarily the achievement thereof.

The deputy agents subtest of the second revision of the familial test proved to be positively related to the equivalent subtests in all the other tests. There was no obvious rationale for this finding. On the one hand, it seemed reasonable to think of defence mechanisms as discrete patterns of behaviour with no necessary relationships with each other. On the other hand, clinical theory suggested the likelihood that the individual might acquire a generalized tendency towards defensiveness in situations that produce insecurity, in which case it could be expected that deputy agents subtests in different tests would be positively related. The assumption of a generalized defensiveness thus offers one explanation of the positive relationship that was found; but there is another explanation. If it may be assumed that insecurity in one area of adjustment is positively related to insecurity in other areas, and since defence mechanisms are positively related to insecurity in that they provide an incomplete defence against it, it is reasonable to find a positive statistical relationship between one deputy agents subtest and another.

The third revision of the familial test included the items of the second revision which had proved to be internally consistent, and added new items to cover two additional mechanisms: (a) over-conscientiousness, which is a generalized manifestation of over-conformity to parents' standards and has a similar rationale; and (b) shallowness in relations with the parents, which is a defence observed clinically as a response to early and profound insecurity in parent-child relations, and which is characterized by a general incapacity for deep and meaningful interpersonal relations generally.

In summary, the items constituting the deputy agents subtest are meant to cover five chief mechanisms: (a) procrastination; (b) over-conformity to parents' standards; (c) rebellion against authority; (d) over-conscientiousness and (e) shallowness in relations with parents.

Item Analysis of the Third Revision of the Familial Test

The first consideration in the item analysis of the new revision was to examine the frequency of endorsements of the "true," "false," and "cannot say" answers (see Table I). At this stage in the analysis, attention was directed to the "true" answers. The criterion was that an item should not be answered "true" by more than 79 per cent or fewer than 10 per cent of the sample population. According to this criterion, all of the items of the independent security, immature dependent security and deputy agents subtests are satisfactory. In the insecurity subtest, items 31 and 32 are earmarked for discard because of too few answers.

On the whole, the frequency of "true" answers to the insecurity items was much lower than expected. Items that had been carried over unchanged from the second revision were answered "true" by a much smaller percentage of the new than of the old sample; items that had been revised with the intention of making them less extreme were answered "true" by an equal or smaller percentage of the new sample than of the sample used for the analysis of the second revision. We are inclined to believe that this difference between the samples is due to

TABLE I

ITEM ANALYSIS OF FAMILIAL TEST (THIRD REVISION) SHOWING COEFFICIENTS OF INTERNAL CONSISTENCY AND PERCENTAGES OF "TRUE," "FALSE" AND "CANNOT SAY" ANSWERS

Subtest	Item	r	% "True"	% "False"	% "Cannot say"
Independent	1	.43	69.7	20.6	9.7
Security	2	.63	48.0	36.0	16.0
	6	.47	35.4	43.4	21.2
	15	.49	33.2	53.7	13.1
	20	.50	77.7	15.4	6.8
	36	.45	39.4	44.6	16.0
Immature	3	.52	24.0	63.4	12.6
Dependent	7	.51	27.4	57.2	15.4
Security	16	.53	45.7	38.3	16.0
	19	.45	17.7	73.7	8.6
	25	.70	34.3	52.0	13.7
	26	.41	37.1	53.7	9.1
Deputy	5	.39	26.9	66.9	6.3
Agents	9	.59	17.1	74.9	8.0
	10	.23	12.0	78.9	9.1
	13	.28	43.4	49.2	7.4
	14	.29	41.7	52.6	5.7
	21	.50	73.7	20.0	6.3
	22	.33	44.6	47.4	8.0
	28	.09	21.7	64.6	13.7
	29	.41	30.9	58.3	10.9
	33	.40	71.4	19.4	9.2
	34	.47	53.8	29.1	17.1
	35	.16	28.6	56.0	15.4
Insecurity	4	.52	39.4	56.6	4.0
	8	.71	20.0	73.1	6.9
	11	.41	14.9	74.3	10.9
	12	.41	14.3	81.7	4.0
	17	.40	18.8	76.6	4.6
	18	.46	18.3	74.3	7.4
	23	.37	10.3	83.4	6.3
	24	.27	28.6	62.9	8.6
	27	.32	13.7	77.7	8.6
	30	.50	10.9	82.3	6.8
	31	.55	4.0	89.2	6.8
	32	.00	4.6	92.0	3.4

a cultural difference between the Canadian university students tested with the second revision of the test and the English university students tested with the third revision. The difference was particularly marked with respect to items reflecting friction with the parents over the question of emancipation; this type of friction seems less frequent among the English students.

Table I also presents the internal consistency coefficients for each item. All the items in the independent and immature dependent security subtests are satisfactory in meeting the criterion of .30. The insecurity subtest is satisfactory on the whole with only items 24 and 32 failing to meet the criterion. Both of these were new items, intended to reflect fear of loss of dependence.

The deputy agents subtest does not come out so well, with only seven of the twelve items meeting the criterion. Of the five mechanisms represented (see page 21), three were covered by the satisfactory items, namely, over-conformity to parents' standards, over-conscientiousness and rebellion against authority. The new items intended to reflect shallowness in relations with the parents were unsatisfactory. Also unsatisfactory were the items dealing with procrastination, although these had proved to be very satisfactory in previous versions of the test. It is believed that another cultural difference between the English and the Canadian samples may be involved here. The two items—13 and 14—are not recommended for discard if the test is to be used with a Canadian population, since they both approximate the criterion very closely, with coefficients of .28 and .29 respectively.

Taking both criteria into account, six items are recommended for discard from the test, namely, items 10, 24, 28, 31, 32 and 35. In addition, it is recommended that items 13 and 14 be discarded if the test is to be used with an English population.

IV SECURITY IN EXTRA-FAMILIAL INTIMACIES

Our preliminary discussion of theory did not make explicit the rationale upon which a test of security and insecurity in extra-familial intimacies should be based. It is, therefore, proposed to begin our consideration of the extra-familial test by extending the basic theory to cover this area of adjustment specifically; we shall make particular reference to security, and defer the discussion of insecurity and deputy agents until later.

Security in extra-familial intimacies fulfils a very important function in adult adjustment. There are limits to the extent to which the person can satisfy his needs through his own efforts. Even the most competent person requires the help, co-operation, and support of others if he is to satisfy those basic physiological needs which are necessary for survival. Yet there is every reason to believe that he requires close relations with his fellows to satisfy more than these basic physiological needs, and that such a need may be experienced in connection with persons who are not directly involved in helping him to survive. A completely independent adjustment is not possible; but even if it were possible, insecurity would ensue through deprivation of these close relations with others. The person needs to belong. The independence that results from the formation of skills and from emancipation from the parents will be insecure unless the person can establish a sure sense of belonging in his relations with others.

There is considerable disagreement about the origins of a need for interpersonal relations. Some believe that it is innate in man. Others believe that it is a secondary, or derived, need. According to the latter, the infant gradually develops a need for his mother because it is through her that his basic physiological needs are satisfied; this need becomes more or less autonomous in relation to the basic needs from which it stemmed and is generalized to people other than the mother. But despite disagreement on origins, there is a consensus that the need for interpersonal relations is strong and important in the human species and that it is first manifested in relations with the parents, especially with the mother.

At the same time that the young child is forming skills that provide the basis for a rudimentary independence, he gradually finds satisfaction in relations with people other than his mother, extending these first to the father and other members of his immediate family and then to adults and children outside the family. He tends at first to establish dependent relationships similar to those he has built up, or would like to build up, with his own parents; this is especially true of his relationships with adults and older children. The less successful he is in achieving independent security, the more likely he is to continue to be immaturely dependent in his extra-familial relations as well as in his familial relations. He expects and needs help, support, advice, and, perhaps especially, affection and approval from his friends as well as from his parents. His orientation is essentially recipient; he expects to receive but is not prepared to give in return. He has achieved immature dependent security if he can rely upon receiving from his friends the help and support he seeks. But many who seek to achieve security through immature dependence fail to do so, and are constantly disappointed that other people do not give the desired affection and support. Moreover, immature dependent security in extra-familial, as in familial, relations tends to be a vulnerable adjustment. If the parents are unable or unwilling to provide unlimited affection, support, and help, other people are likely to be even more unable and unwilling to do so. Immature dependent security collapses if the agent upon whom the person depends is removed or withdraws his support.

A mature basis of dependent security implies something beyond a purely recipient relationship; it involves a mutual dependence of two people, both of them contributing and both receiving. There is no incompatibility between mature dependent security in extra-familial intimacies and independent security in other areas of adjustment. Indeed, these are supplementary. Mature dependent security helps to fill the gaps that cannot be covered by independence. On the other hand, some degree of independent security is necessary for both persons in a relationship of mutual dependence, for each in his own measure is responsible for providing support for the other.

It is not immediately clear what constitutes independent security in extra-familial relations. The development of the rationale of independent security is an important aspect of the discussion of the three versions of the test which will be considered now.

The First Extra-Familial Test

The first extra-familial test (10, 11) consisted of two scales, one measuring security-insecurity and the other measuring tolerance-intolerance. Intolerance was considered to be a defence mechanism pertinent to extra-familial adjustment, and thus the scale was intended to provide a measure of defensiveness even though only one mechanism was represented. Further consideration will be given to this scale in a later section when deputy agents are discussed.

In the scale designed to measure security-insecurity no distinction was made between independent, mature dependent and immature dependent security. An examination of the items suggested that the scale reflected independent rather than dependent security, since most of them dealt with self-confidence and social skills. Case studies indicated that this scale provided an inadequate coverage of security in the extra-familial area. Included among the subjects classified as secure by the test were some who were shown by other methods of appraisal to be incapable of close interpersonal relations; they tended to compensate for this by joining organizations and "running things," and generally tried to substitute status and recognition for mutual dependence in their relations with others. Although the underlying theory holds that mature dependent security is the most desirable mode of adjustment in extra-familial relations, this view was not reflected by the first test. Instead, an emphasis upon independent security had been introduced, perhaps because of unwarranted generalization from other areas in which independent security was considered to be the most satisfactory mode of adjustment.

The First Revision of the Extra-Familial Test

Experience with the first extra-familial test pointed to the need to clarify the role played by skills and self-confidence in extra-familial relations, and the place of the "independent solution" in this area of adjustment. As a first step it seemed desirable to distinguish between the competitive, status-seeking aspects and the dependent aspects of interpersonal relations. Skill and self-confidence seem to be more closely involved with the competitive aspects than with the dependent aspects, and, because competitive striving is believed to be a manifestation of insecurity, it cannot be postulated that competitive skills result in security. Indeed success in competition does not necessarily bring security to the person who wins it for he has no assurance that he will continue to surpass all challengers, and there will be continuing insecurity if he needs constantly to reinforce his position of superiority. A person can be said to be secure in competitive activity only in the sense that he values the activity for its own sake, and not because it brings him success and increased status. Security of this sort is compatible with mature dependent security in extra-familial relations, but status-seeking is incompatible both with the co-operative, give-and-take relations of mature intimacies and with the helpless, recipient orientation characteristic of immature dependence.

The purpose of the first revision of the extra-familial test was to explore the distinction between the competitive and the dependency aspects of extra-familial relations outlined in the above rationale. To this end, two tests were developed, a test of "belonging" constructed by Whitehouse (14) and a test of "competition" constructed by Walter (13). Both tests were intended to cover the entire range of interpersonal relations, from the closest to the most distant, and therefore some items referring to familial relations were included. Because of this it is inaccurate to state that these two tests together constitute the first revision of the extra-familial test, but it is convenient to do so since they were intended to clarify the rationale of security in extra-familial relations.

In her test of "competition" Walter distinguished between two types: "formal" and "informal." Formal competition is competition under agreed conditions and rules, such as that found in organized sports and games. Within the framework of rules, the secure person can enjoy his skills for their own sake without feeling driven to maintain his status. In the "informal" situation, where competition is not implicit in the structure of the situation itself, the secure person is noncompetitive in his attitudes, and any stress on competition indicates insecurity.

Walter's test included four subtests, measuring independent security, immature dependent security, deputy agents, and insecurity. The independent security subtest was intended to reflect an enjoyment of the skills and activities involved in a competitive situation, with a lack of concern about status and, hence, about winning or losing. In a formal competitive situation the secure person may exert competitive effort and find enjoyment therein without seeking status; in the informal situation he abandons all competitive attitudes. The items which met the criteria of internal consistency have implicit in them a definition of independent security approximating the underlying rationale fairly closely, but they also reflect a conventional ideal of good sportsmanship. It is believed that a person could pay lip-service to this conventional ideal by endorsing the items, while still feeling considerable underlying concern regarding status—a concern incompatible with independent security.

Immature dependent security is defined by the items of that subtest as an evasion of competitive situations. Sports or games are undertaken only under conditions where status does not matter and the competitive element does not play a part. There is the further implication that it would be preferable to accept an unpleasant situation than to assert oneself competitively in order to avoid the unpleasantness. It is believed that these items could be endorsed by a person so dependent on others that he dares not risk any competitive undertaking for fear of jeopardizing his relations with them and losing their affection. This response seems to be related to the mechanics of sustaining an immature dependent security rather than to the security itself. The subtest yielded a J-shaped curve, since few of the sample population endorsed any of the items of the subtest.

Both the independent and the immature dependent security subtests of this revision imply that security in competition is attained only by avoiding a competitive attitude. This common factor perhaps explains the highly significant positive statistical relationship that was found between the two subtests. Nonetheless, doubt is cast upon the validity of the subtests by the strong relationship between them, because the underlying theory requires that a clear-cut distinction be made by the subtests between independent and immature dependent security.

Whitehouse's test of "belonging" included four subtests, dealing with mature dependent security, immature dependent security, deputy agents and insecurity. Only the first two of these subtests will be considered here. In each of the subtests three levels of relationship were distinguished—with intimates, acquaintances, and "contacts."

The items of the mature dependent security subtest dealt with the satisfaction obtained by the individual in his relations with other people, including parents, other members of the immediate family, relatives, class-mates, and people with whom only casual contacts were made. It is difficult to understand how the concept of mature dependent security was intended to apply in relations with the last group because satisfactions derived from such relations seem to reflect a gregarious kind of sociability involving an immature kind of dependence on other people. This is probably the explanation of the significant positive statistical correlations that were found between this subtest and the immature dependent security subtests of the familial "belonging" and "competition" tests. All the items of the mature dependent security subtest that met the criterion of internal consistency could be endorsed by a person with an exaggerated need for affection and approval who is essentially recipient in his orientation and, hence, immaturely dependent.

The items of the immature dependent security subtest also reflected dependence on others for affection, support, help and approval. The chief defect of the subtest was that the items involved an immature dependent orientation rather than *security* obtained through such an orientation. Moreover, the endorsements yielded a J-shaped curve, and represented a form of immature dependence too extreme to be applicable to more than a very few in the sample population.

The Second Revision of the Extra-Familial Test

The second revision of the extra-familial test represented a considerable departure from the two earlier versions. Valuable experience was gained through work with the first test and the experimental revision thereof, but the application of this experience in constructing the second revision was indirect. Most of the subtests of the previous versions failed to reflect the basic theory of security in extra-familial relations and few of the items could be used in the new version even with changes of wording. In the second revision there are no separate tests of belonging and competition; both aspects of extra-familial relations are dealt with in one test, with more emphasis on belonging than on competition. The distinction made by Whitehouse between different degrees of intimacy is no longer made. Most of the items of the new test refer by implication to intimacies, but some of them, especially in the independent security subtest, may be interpreted to refer to social relationships other than intimacies. The new test makes no distinction between formal and informal competitive situations, but by implication the items refer to informal social situations. In the second revision all items are concerned with extra-familial relations.

There are five subtests in this version of the extra-familial test: independent security, mature dependent security, immature dependent security, insecurity and deputy agents. The items of the test may be seen in the Appendix, grouped according to subtest.

Independent Security

· The first extra-familial test implied that independent security consisted of self-confidence resting upon social skills. The definition given in Walter's test of competition was that independent security was an enjoyment of the exercise of skills in a competitive situation with lack of concern about gaining or losing status as an outcome of competitive effort. In planning the present revision of the extra-familial test it was decided that a combination of these two definitions would provide an adequate rationale for the independent security subtest, and would ensure a distinction between it and the immature dependent security subtest which Walter's test failed to make. Independent security in extra-familial relations is thus defined as self-confidence in social situations, resting at least in part upon skills, with enough satisfaction in the status given by these skills that status is not a matter for concern.

The concept of "status" requires further discussion, since although it is a central concept here, it has not yet been considered except in the context of formally competitive situations where it is determined by the outcome of the competition in terms of winning or losing. In informal situations—and the second revision of the test is concerned only with these—the individual evaluates his own status in the social group by any one or any combinations of a variety of criteria, such as quantity and quality of possessions, money, educational level, prestige value of his occupation, "blue-book" ranking, and skills. Of these criteria, only abilities or skills are considered pertinent to independent security. If the person's status depends upon his own skills, it obviously depends upon what he has been able to achieve through his own efforts, and in this sense he is independent. Yet, even in cases where status rests on skills, the person is insecure or potentially insecure as long as his status in the group is a matter of concern to him, because there is the ever-present threat that others may surpass him in degree of skill. For this reason the definition of the independently secure person specifies that he is unconcerned about his status. Furthermore, it is assumed that only a person who has at least fair status can feel unconcerned. In our culture the competitive and status-seeking aspects of interpersonal relations are so emphasized that it is difficult to imagine a person so secure that he would feel no concern about having a very low status in the social groups to which he belongs. Therefore, the definition of the independently secure person includes the specification that it is because he is satisfied with his status that status is of no concern to him; the implication is that he has some reasonable degree of status or else he would not be satisfied. The items of the subtest mention only skills as a basis for status, but it is recognized that other factors, perhaps more closely related to dependent than to independent security, may contribute to the status of the person, whether he recognizes them or not. Finally, it seems very likely that status would be a matter of unconcern only to the person who has a secure sense of belonging in his intimate relationships, and therefore it may be expected that the independently secure person will also have mature dependent security in his extra-familial relations. Because of this, independent security may be considered a supplement to mature dependent security, but not a substitute for it.

It was not possible to include in all items all components of the definition of independent security, namely, self-confidence in social situations, self-confidence resting on skills, satisfaction with status and lack of concern regarding status. No item includes more than two of these components, but the subtest as a whole was designed to include all components. None of the items of the previous versions of the test was considered suitable and, hence, all the items of the independent security subtest of the second revision are new.

Mature Dependent Security

Little need be said here about the rationale of the subtest intended to measure mature dependent security in extra-familial relations, since it remains unchanged. Security of this sort is believed to come through the sense of warmth and belonging derived from participation in an interdependent, mutually contributing relationship. In framing the items it was believed to be undesirable to give direct expression to this definition, since it conforms so closely to the social and moral ideal. It could be expected that items emphasizing a mutually contributing relationship would be endorsed by too many people, some of whom merely hold this kind of a relationship as an ideal. Instead of emphasizing a give-and-take relationship, several items of the subtest specifically disclaim the "take" aspect in stating that the person is not concerned with the response he receives from others. It was hoped that this kind of item would overcome the defect of this subtest as it appeared in Whitehouse's test of belonging, the items of which were endorsed by persons so preoccupied by obtaining a warm response from others that they could be classed only as immaturely dependent. All the items of the present version of the mature dependent security subtest are new.

Immature Dependent Security

The rationale for the immature dependent security subtest remains essentially the same. The immature dependently secure person is defined as one who relies upon his friends for help, advice, affection, and approval, who has a marked need for the emotional support of other people and is successful in having this need met, and who tends to maintain this dependently secure adjustment by efforts to please and to avoid offending the people upon whom he is dependent. In phrasing the items emphasis was placed upon the satisfaction obtained from dependence on others, not merely upon the fact that such dependence exists. Since Whitehouse's immature dependent security failed to give this emphasis, it was possible to use only one of his items, and that one was reworded.

Insecurity

Insecurity in extra-familial relations is characterized primarily by feelings of loneliness and isolation resulting from a failure to satisfy the need to form close relationships with other people. It was this primary type of insecurity that was emphasized in the insecurity subtest of Whitehouse's test of belonging.

There are two chief ways of handling this primary insecurity, which in themselves may result in a secondary type of insecurity. One way is to make a special effort to win the liking, approval, and emotional support of others and thus to gain immature dependent security. The other way is to try to win the admiration and respect of others through achievements. To the extent to which the person enjoys the process of learning the new skills necessary for achievement, he builds up a basis of independent security through his efforts. To the extent to which his satisfactions rest upon the regard won from other people as a result of his achievements, his need for achievement is compensatory and a defence mechanism. Failure in either of these two types of effort brings a secondary insecurity, which seems similar in kind to the primary insecurity that gave rise to the efforts in the first place.

The insecurity items of the first version of the extra-familial test reflected both of these secondary forms of insecurity, but emphasized insecurity resulting from failure to win approval through skill and achievement. Inadequate emphasis was given to primary isolation and lack of belonging. Walter's insecurity subtest placed its entire emphasis on failure in winning security through achievement; all the items reflected fear of loss of status, whether directly or indirectly.

In order to reflect both primary insecurity and the two secondary forms of insecurity three sets of items were planned for the second revision of the insecurity subtest: (*a*) items reflecting an unhappy feeling of loneliness, isolation, and lack of closeness and warmth; (*b*) items reflecting uneasy feelings of being disliked and disapproved of, implying failure of the person's efforts to gain immature dependent security; and (*c*) items reflecting feelings of failure in gaining status, uneasiness in competitive situations and lack of self-confidence in social situations, implying failure of the person's efforts to win regard through achievement.

This revision abandoned Walter's distinction between formal and informal competitive situations and Whitehouse's distinction between various degrees of intimacy in interpersonal relations. The items of their subtests were therefore unsuitable for the present revision, despite the fact that they had met the expectations of the rationale in statistical inter-test comparisons. Furthermore, the items of their subtests were so extreme that few of them were endorsed frequently enough to meet the criterion for retention. Therefore all the items are new in the present version of the subtest.

Deputy Agents

In the first extra-familial test the use of deputy agents was measured by a scale supplementary to the security-insecurity scale, a scale of "tolerance-intolerance." The items indicating intolerance dealt with attitudes revealed in such actions as excluding strangers from the group, seeking to associate with people of higher status, being over-critical, and quarrelling with others.

Walter's subtest dealing with deputy agents limited itself entirely to attitudes towards status since it dealt with competition. Her rationale implies that it is a defence mechanism to place a high value upon status. The items proved to be infrequently endorsed, few of them meeting the criterion of 10 per cent endorsement.

In Whitehouse's test of belonging the deputy agent subtest dealt with mechanisms used by the person to defend himself against feeling alone and isolated: these ranged from rationalizing that the isolated state is desirable to the creation of imaginary companions. Very few of the items met the criterion of 10 per cent endorsement. (The subtest proved to have a significant positive relationship with the immature dependent security subtest. This supported our opinion that the latter over-emphasized the mechanics of maintaining a dependent position and under-emphasized feelings of security.)

It is believed that the items of these subtests of the first revision were infrequently endorsed because not enough care was taken in phrasing the items; the mechanism in question must seem "natural" enough and acceptable enough to the subject who employs it that he will admit that he does so—provided, of course, that he is aware that he employs it. In framing the items of the second revision of the subtest an attempt was made to avoid this fault. Furthermore, an attempt was made to formulate a more explicit rationale for the subtest.

The chief function of deputy agents in extra-familial relations is to protect the person from feelings of isolation or from fear that he will become isolated through loss of the affection or regard others now have for him. The most extreme defence is the same as that which arises in early childhood as a result of extreme deprivation of affection and consequent failure to achieve any appreciable degree of dependent security in familial relations. The defensive manœuvre is, in essence, a withdrawal from close relations to the extent that there is interference with the normal development of a need for close relations with others. This results in an essential shallowness of relations. The child views other people only as instruments for the satisfaction of other needs, with no concern for affection, approval, and belonging. It is believed that this orientation then tends to carry over into all subsequent interpersonal relationships.

Other mechanisms arise later as defences against secondary insecurity in interpersonal relations. These mechanisms fall into two chief classes. First, some mechanisms serve to provide a substitute for a sense of belonging or to reinforce whatever feelings of belonging the person already experiences. In the second revision of the subtest the following mechanisms of this type were represented: emphasis upon status and achievement, snobbishness, conformity to avoid disapproval, and the substitution of participation in organized groups for a real sense of belonging in intimate relationships. Secondly, there are other mechanisms that protect the person from feeling hurt in his relations with others by increasing his isolation from them. In the second revision of the subtest two such mechanisms are included—withdrawal and hostility.

Three items of the revised subtest were taken from previous versions, one from the immature dependent security subtest of Whitehouse's test of belonging, and two from the tolerance-intolerance scale of the first test; both of these dealt with snobbishness.

In summary, the deputy agents subtest of the second revision of the extra-familial test consists of items intended to cover the following seven mechanisms of defence: (*a*) shallowness in extra-familial relations; (*b*) emphasis on status and achievement; (*c*) snobbishness; (*d*) conformity in order to avoid disapproval; (*e*) substitution of

TABLE II

Subtest	Item	r	% "True"	% "False"	% "Cannot say"
Independent	2	.56	44.0	36.0	20.0
Security	8	.40	74.3	14.9	10.9
	17	.41	75.4	12.6	12.0
	24	.66	54.3	32.0	13.7
	34	.55	28.6	53.7	17.7
	36	.47	39.4	37.2	23.4
Mature	1	.40	25.7	54.3	20.0
Dependent	9	.30	34.3	46.3	19.4
Security	16	.44	85.7	12.6	1.7
	25	.41	63.4	25.2	11.4
	35	.52	52.0	38.9	9.1
	39	.45	78.9	14.9	6.3
Immature	3	.41	41.7	38.9	19.4
Dependent	4	.19	24.0	56.0	20.0
Security	10	.56	33.7	56.0	10.3
	18	.65	42.9	40.0	17.1
	19	.53	40.6	41.7	17.7
	26	.52	68.5	22.9	8.6
Deputy	6	.47	34.9	51.4	13.7
Agents	7	.28	21.2	52.0	26.9
	13	.43	33.2	54.9	12.0
	14	.27	19.4	74.9	5.7
	15	.37	18.9	68.6	12.6
	20	.40	17.1	74.9	8.0
	21	.29	18.8	72.6	8.6
	29	.12	53.7	34.3	12.0
	30	.32	13.7	77.7	8.6
	31	.37	38.3	53.7	8.0
	32	.23	13.7	73.7	12.6
	33	.10	4.0	88.6	7.4
Insecurity	5	.56	56.6	33.7	9.7
	11	.39	41.7	47.4	10.9
	12	.44	10.3	80.5	9.2
	22	.35	14.3	81.7	4.0
	23	.39	26.9	68.1	5.1
	27	.42	48.0	37.1	14.9
	28	.52	34.9	54.3	10.9
	37	.61	36.6	53.7	9.7
	38	.40	60.6	30.9	8.6
	40	.40	29.7	59.4	10.9
	41	.40	20.6	73.1	6.3
	42	.51	22.9	65.7	11.4

participation in organized groups for belonging in intimate relationships; (f) withdrawal and (g) hostility.

Item Analysis of the Second Revision of the Extra-Familial Test

The percentages of "true," "false," and "cannot say" answers to the items of the second revision of the extra-familial test are shown in Table II. According to the criterion that an item is unsatisfactory if the "true" answer is endorsed by more than 79 per cent or fewer than 10 per cent, two items are earmarked for discard—item 16 in the mature dependent security subtest, which is too frequently endorsed, and item 33 in the deputy agents subtest, which is too infrequently endorsed. With respect to this criterion the second revision is a great improvement over the first revision of the test.

In Table II are also shown the coefficients of internal consistency for each item, which give the correlation of the item with the subtest to which it has been assigned. All the items of the independent security, mature dependent security and insecurity subtests meet the criterion of internal consistency satisfactorily, nearly all being well above the criterion of .30. One item of the immature dependent security subtest—item 4—is earmarked for discard. As in the case of the familial test, it is the deputy agents subtest that is least satisfactory, with six of the twelve items having coefficients below .30—items 7, 14, 21, 29, 32 and 33. Nevertheless, the mechanisms mentioned on page 34 are represented by at least one remaining item except for "withdrawal," which was represented only by item 33.

Thus, except for the deputy agents subtest, the item analysis shows the extra-familial test to be satisfactory in terms of frequency of endorsements and internal consistency.

V SECURITY IN AVOCATIONS

Security in avocations may be defined simply as the enjoyment of time that is free from work and routine tasks. In states of independent and mature dependent security this enjoyment is based upon the acquisition and exercise of skills. The person in either of these states plays an actively participant role, in contrast with the state of immature dependent security where the role is one of a passive spectator. With independent security the person's active participation is independent of the presence and co-operation of other people. With either mature or immature dependent security, the person bases his security upon other people. With mature dependent security he derives enjoyment from activities in which one or more other people participate with him. With immature dependent security he requires other people to be active in providing entertainment that he enjoys passively. Insecurity in avocations is characterized chiefly by feelings of boredom. Defence mechanisms pertinent to avocations are of two main kinds: those arising from the person's need to escape boredom, and those arising from insecurity in other areas of adjustment that intrude upon the person's use of his spare time.

Both the first avocational test and the present revision thereof were based upon the rationale that is briefly stated above. It is proposed to discuss them together with respect to each of the five subtests, giving a somewhat expanded statement of the rationale for each subtest. The items of the first test are not shown here, but the items of the revision may be seen in the Appendix.

Independent Security

The independently secure person acts as his own agent for providing enjoyment of whatever time he does not need to spend in work and routine activities. Because of the economic organization of our culture it is very difficult for the person to achieve independent security in his occupation. Avocations are the chief area of adjustment in which he can be free from dependence on other people and yet be secure. Avocations therefore assume an importance in contributing to the individual's over-all security beyond the level that might be assumed from a superficial view.

In constructing both the first test and the revision, it was considered very important to give a positive definition to independence in avocational pursuits. The independent security does not imply a denial of enjoying other people, or a withdrawal from social interaction, or an escape from the real world into an inner life of fantasy. To avoid these implications the items of the independent security subtest emphasize an *activity* that is enjoyable whether other people are present or not, rather than enjoyment of time spent *alone*.

With respect to the statistical criteria, Styffe's version of the independent security subtest (see p. ix) proved to be remarkably satisfactory for a first attempt. Eight items of her subtest met the criteria for retention in terms of percentage endorsement and internal consistency. The subtest was found to be positively related both to independent security in the familial area and to mature dependent security in the philosophical area, in accordance with the rationale. The fact that it was not positively related to independent security in Walter's test of competition was considered to be a fault of the latter. The faults in the first version of the subtest were minor ones: the items were phrased in academic language and some of them seemed to reflect an air of self-conscious virtue. Perhaps because of these minor faults the percentage endorsements tended to be low, although still above the criterion of 10 per cent.

The first revision of the subtest retained the same definition of independent security, namely, enjoyment of spare time through active participation in pursuits requiring skill or creativity, independent of the co-operation of other people. As in the first version, the emphasis was upon active participation rather than upon non-social aspects. Only one item of the subtest is new. Two items were taken over from the previous test without change, while three were reworded slightly.

Mature Dependent Security

Independent security and mature dependent security are by no means incompatible, since both are based on an enjoyment of activities requiring skill. To be sure, some activities, such as games and organized sports, require the co-operation of two or more persons, and others, such as writing poetry and cabinet making, are best undertaken singly. But the attitude of the secure person is the same—an actively participant one. Therefore, the expectation is that there will be a significant positive statistical relationship between the independent and mature dependent security subtests.

The first version of the mature dependent security subtest proved to have no significant relationship with the independent security subtest. On the contrary, it was found to have significant positive statistical relations with those subtests of the familial and extra-familial tests that reflected immature dependence. The inference is that the first version of the subtest reflects a strong need for belonging to a group and for gaining the approval of and status within that group. An examination of the items suggested that the reason for these unexpected relationships with other subtests was that the items emphasized skills and activities as they contributed to the enjoyment of the group rather than to the individual's enjoyment of the participation itself.

Before revising the avocational test, consideration was given to the elimination of the mature dependent security subtest on the grounds that it overlapped with the mature dependent security subtest of the extra-familial test. It was decided that there was not enough overlap to justify elimination. Mature dependent security in avocations is based upon the enjoyment of activities in a social context, whereas mature dependent security in extra-familial intimacies is based on feelings of warmth and belonging achieved through mutually contributing relations with others. A person who lacks close and satisfactory intimate relations with others, may nevertheless enjoy participation in group activity. Mature dependent security in avocations may thus be a healthy and helpful form of compensation for a relative lack of mature dependent security in intimacies.

All the items of the revised subtest are new. They are phrased to emphasize the enjoyment of participation with other people, rather than to imply that it is important for the person to please the group. It was thus hoped to overcome the faults of the first version.

Immature Dependent Security

Immature dependent security in avocations may be either social or non-social. The person is in a state of immature dependent security when he enjoys listening to the radio by himself, when he enjoys the theatre in the company of other people, and when he enjoys the conversation of a group without participating in it. The factor common to these situations is that in them the person enjoys the role of passive spectator.

It may be argued that the person need not be passive in these situations, and that an effort to understand and to appreciate implies some participation. Moreover, he may enjoy spectator activity as a facet of a participant interest in sports, music, theatre and the like. For this reason, it was considered important when framing items to make explicit a passive orientation.

Six items of the subtest constructed by Styffe proved to be satisfactory in meeting the criteria of percentage endorsement and internal consistency. As required by the rationale, the subtest as a whole had significant positive statistical relationships with the subtest of other tests which reflected immature dependence on other people. On the other hand, it had a highly significant positive relationship with the deputy agents subtest of the avocational test; this suggests a fault in either or both of these subtests.

Despite the fact that the first version of the subtest seemed to be successful in reflecting a passive orientation, most of the items were limited in application, since they dealt with specific situations in which the person played the role of a spectator. In revising the subtest the items were given a more general application, and more emphasis was placed upon *enjoyment* of the spectator role in the hope of reducing the overlap with the deputy agents subtest. Four of the items are entirely new, and the other two were taken from the previous version of the subtest with slight revision.

Insecurity

When a person is bored in his spare time he is insecure. He experiences a generalized state of restlessness, and is unable to find satisfaction for his needs for perceptual and motor activity. Boredom is difficult to tolerate, yet it is readily alleviated through a change of activity. If the person is still restless and bored after such a change, it may be suspected that his state of boredom is reinforced by generalized tension arising from insecurity in some other area of adjustment. Prolonged boredom is uncommon and probably indicates acute insecurity in enough aspects of the person's adjustment that he may be described as generally insecure.

The items of the first version of the insecurity subtest referred to chronic rather than occasional boredom. This was perhaps the reason that they proved to be infrequently endorsed. Only four items met the criteria for retention, but these four, taken together, met the requirements of the rationale. They were substantially related to the insecurity subtests of other tests, and also to three of the subtests dealing with deputy agents. Three of these items were incorporated into the revised subtest without change and one with slight revision. The other eight items are new.

The new items are intended to reflect boredom that is less intense and less generalized than that reflected by the first version of the subtest. This intent was expressed in three ways. Some items specified that boredom was occasional or frequent but not constant. Some items referred to tension and restlessness that the subject might not himself characterize as boredom. Some items described the subject as one who does not particularly enjoy his spare-time pursuits, but made no specific reference to boredom. Thus, insecurity in the avocational area is defined by the items as boredom (even though it be only occasional), tension, restlessness, and failure to derive real enjoyment from spare-time activities.

Deputy Agents

The mechanisms of defence dealt with by this subtest are of two types. Some mechanisms are specifically defences against boredom. Others have been developed to protect the person against insecurity in other areas of adjustment, but are included here because they intrude upon the use of spare time.

Both types of mechanism are represented in the items of the first version of the subtest. The items that met the criterion of internal consistency covered a search for excitement as a way of escaping troubles, rationalizations for failure to develop satisfying spare-time interests, and a too-serious use of spare time. The items of the subtest were so infrequently endorsed that none met the criterion of 10 per cent. Therefore, all items of the revised version of the subtest are new.

The first consideration in revising the subtest was to frame the items in such a way as to encourage more frequent endorsements. An attempt was also made to distinguish between mechanisms serving as specific defences against avocational insecurity and those protecting against insecurity arising in other areas, but this was found to be difficult. Two mechanisms seem to belong clearly to the latter class. One is characterized by a need for success, approval, or status which intrudes into spare-time activities and prevents the person from using his spare-time primarily for his own enjoyment. A second consists of an over-emphasis on spare-time activities as an escape from facing the demands of reality in other areas of adjustment.

The other mechanisms represented in the new version of the subtest might have arisen either as specific defences against avocational insecurity or as defences against insecurity in other areas. These are as follows: excitement as an escape from boredom, reliance upon artificial stimulation to bolster enjoyment, rationalizations for not developing

TABLE III

Item Analysis of Avocational Test (First Revision) Showing Coefficients of Internal Consistency and Percentages of "True," "False," and "Cannot Say" Answers

Subtest	Item	r	% "True"	% "False"	% "Cannot say"
Independent	2	.39	85.1	4.6	10.3
Security	11	.47	68.6	23.4	8.0
	16	.52	84.6	9.1	6.3
	17	.49	80.6	9.7	9.7
	24	.38	78.9	14.3	6.8
	29	.49	72.0	19.4	8.6
Mature	1	.56	46.3	45.7	8.0
Dependent	12	.53	33.1	54.3	12.6
Security	18	.60	58.9	33.1	8.0
	19	.56	45.7	37.7	16.6
	34	.70	49.1	40.0	10.9
	39	.70	29.7	55.4	14.9
Immature	3	.47	48.0	38.3	13.7
Dependent	13	.63	16.6	68.5	14.9
Security	15	.41	33.1	50.3	16.6
	25	.45	36.0	51.4	12.6
	26	.32	42.3	34.9	22.9
	30	.50	38.9	50.3	10.9
Deputy	6	.06	17.7	65.7	16.6
Agents	7	.33	28.6	61.1	10.3
	8	.32	30.3	61.7	8.0
	20	.47	19.4	68.1	12.6
	21	.56	25.7	66.3	8.0
	27	.45	32.0	56.6	11.4
	28	.43	20.0	70.8	9.2
	32	.40	44.6	45.1	10.3
	33	.30	15.4	78.3	6.3
	37	.22	10.3	84.0	5.7
	38	.33	22.3	70.8	6.9
	41	.43	12.6	78.9	8.6
Insecurity	4	.37	6.9	90.2	2.9
	5	.58	36.6	57.8	5.7
	9	.37	17.7	76.6	5.7
	10	.42	31.4	62.9	5.7
	14	.38	55.4	38.9	5.7
	22	.37	13.7	78.9	7.4
	23	.18	5.1	90.8	4.0
	31	.46	18.3	78.4	3.4
	35	.57	12.0	81.1	6.9
	36	.46	25.7	70.8	3.4
	40	.18	2.9	93.7	3.4
	42	.33	7.4	90.3	2.3

spare-time interests and being too busy to have avocations. The items dealing with the last defence do not make it possible to distinguish the person with such meagre avocational resources that he must fill his spare time with work from the person who is driven by pervasive, generalized anxiety to a press of work.

Item Analysis of the Revised Avocational Test

Table III shows the percentage endorsements of "true," "false," and "cannot say" answers, as well as the coefficients of internal consistency for the items of the avocational test. A great surprise in the item analysis was the very frequent endorsement of the items of the independent security subtest by the sample population. This was unexpected because these items were the same as or very similar to the items of the first version of the subtest that had been endorsed much less frequently by the previous sample. The difference is attributed to a cultural difference between the English sample upon which the present item analysis is based and the Canadian sample with which previous work was done. Items 2, 16, and 17 are endorsed by 80 per cent or more of the new sample, and therefore fail to meet the criterion for retention in the test. Yet all the items of the subtest meet the criterion of internal consistency. It is suggested that no items be discarded from the subtest, at least without further trial, if the test is to be used with a Canadian rather than an English population. It may well be that the Canadian culture offers less encouragement to an independently secure adjustment in avocations than the English culture.

All items in the mature and immature dependent security subtests meet both the criterion of percentage endorsements and the criterion of internal consistency. The deputy agents subtest is also shown to be satisfactory by the item analysis, with only items 6 and 37 failing to meet the criterion of internal consistency.

The revised insecurity subtest did not entirely overcome the difficulty of framing items commonly enough endorsed to be useful. Items 4, 23, 40 and 42 are too infrequently endorsed to be retained, and of these, two fail also to meet the criterion of internal consistency. The eight remaining items give adequate coverage to the three aspects of insecurity that the test was intended to include.

VI SECURITY IN PHILOSOPHY OF LIFE

No matter how secure a person may be in his everyday life, his security will be shaken when he first encounters catastrophe, serious illness, injury, or the possibility of death, whether the threat is directed towards himself or towards other people on whom his security depends. Many such threats are beyond the control of any individual no matter how skilled he may be. Co-operative enterprise on the part of a group of people or the community as a whole may serve to avert or lessen them, but there are limits to human power, and the recognition of these limits brings insecurity.

Insecurity does not arise only when a threat is direct and immediate. Imagination, and especially perhaps the capacity for empathy, extends the person's vulnerability to catastrophe. He may feel insecure when disaster befalls someone else, either because he is able to imagine how he would feel if he were in the place of the other person, or because he suddenly realizes "This could happen to me!"

Much of the history of civilization deals with man's efforts to gain security in the face of threats beyond his power to avert. Established religions may be viewed as providing a way for the individual to achieve security through adherence to prescribed beliefs and practices. As an alternative to accepting one of the traditional orthodoxies, the individual may find security in a philosophy of life that he works out for himself, usually either through a modification of one of the orthodoxies or an adaptation of one of the great philosophical systems to suit his own needs. The basis of the security found by the person in a religious faith may be in allying himself with a divine or supernatural power that transcends the limitations of his own competence. Or the basis of his security may rest upon an increased understanding of his place in the larger scheme of things and an acceptance of the limitations of his understanding and competence. Science, following in the wake of the great philosophies, has greatly extended the limits of human control over natural forces, but the crux of religion and philosophy is to deal with those areas beyond the outside limits of human control. As a concomitant, religion and philosophy, unlike science, almost invariably have a code of behaviour which the individual is exhorted to follow as a guide to action, with the implication that to follow the code contributes either to his own security or to that of society as a whole.

In attempting to assess the extent to which the individual feels secure in his religion or philosophy of life we shall not presume to evaluate different established religions or philosophies in terms of the degree of security they tend to provide or the kind of security offered. It is the attitude of the individual himself with which we are concerned. Among those who adhere to any given established religion there are some who are insecure because they have insufficient faith; there are others who are secure because of an unquestioning, child-like acceptance of the religion in which they have been reared; and there are still others who are secure because they have worked through to a mature acceptance of the orthodox faith. Similarly, among those who reject established religion, there are some who are insecure because they have no faith in anything; there are others who are secure because they have worked out a satisfactory philosophy of their own; and there may be others who are secure in a philosophy of life which they have taken over from some one else in a child-like unquestioning way without having worked it through for themselves.

The focus of our interest in security and insecurity in the religious or philosophical area of adjustment is the individual's feelings about values, morals, life, death, and his place in the larger scheme of things. He may attempt to achieve security by various means but there is one way that is closed to him. He cannot be omniscient or omnipotent. It it only when he has matured to the extent that he realizes the limitations both of his own powers and of those of the persons upon whom he depends or hopes to depend that he experiences the insecurity that gives rise to his need for a philosophy of life. Even then, he may not be led to a concern with religion or philosophy until he encounters a threat severe enough to make him realize the vulnerability of his other bases of security.

The first test of security in the area of philosophy of life was devised by Mrs. Marion Wright and was first administered to a sample population by one of us (L.H.A.) (1). It was then revised in the present study without major changes in the rationale. We propose, therefore, to discuss the two versions of the test at the same time with respect to each of the four subtests. The items of the first test are not shown here, but the items of the revised test may be seen in the Appendix.

Mature Dependent Security

Since independent security is impossible in the philosophical area of the person's life, mature dependent security is believed to be the best possible mode of adjustment. The prototype of mature dependent security occurs in intimate extra-familial relations. The core of the definition of mature dependent security is that the person is secure in his dependence upon a relationship in which he himself contributes. The extension of this definition to the philosophical area requires that the person feel that he belongs, not only in his more or less intimate relationships, but in the world at large, and that the contribution he has to make is somehow significant in the larger scheme of things. This is in contrast to the feeling of insignificance, helplessness, and isolation that characterizes insecurity in the philosophical area.

A philosophy of life capable of being the foundation for a mature and dependently secure adjustment cannot be achieved without effort. It is only in response to a fairly critical degree of insecurity, in which the person's previous bases of security are shaken, that a need for a philosophy of life is felt. One criterion of mature dependent security is that the person has worked through his religious beliefs or philosophy of life and made them truly his own. Only then does he have confidence that his philosophy will stand up against the insecurity that further crises will bring.

Furthermore, it is our opinion that the maturely dependent solution to insecurity in this area implies a continuing goal-directed activity rather than a rigid code of behaviour which, having once been adopted, plays a static role in the person's life. An adequate philosophy of life includes a set of values in terms of which the person guides his behaviour, and thus provides goals towards which he directs his activity. This long-range orientation helps him to tolerate frustrations and to postpone gratifications in the present in the interests of future gratifications that seem more important to him. It is by no means necessary for the person to achieve his goals in order to gain security. He may feel secure through a sense of small gains in his progress towards his eventual goals. The tolerance of insecurity thus acquired is an important aspect of mature dependent security.

The first version of the mature dependent security subtest was intended to reflect the rationale as stated above. Nearly all the items of the subtest met the criterion of internal consistency to a highly satisfactory degree. The subtest as a whole satisfied the expectations of the rationale in most of its relationships with other subtests, but significant positive relationships with the immature dependent security subtest of the philosophical test and with the insecurity subtest of the familial test were quite out of line with expectations. An examination of the items of the mature and immature dependent security subtests of the philosophical test suggested an explanation of the undesirable overlap between them. Both subtests included items dealing with humanitarian values without distinguishing adequately between persons who have worked through to a mature assimilation of these values and those whose conventional religious beliefs lead them to subscribe to the same values even though they are accepted in an immature and unquestioning way. The positive relationship between the mature dependent security subtest of the philosophical test and the insecurity subtest of the familial tests suggests that the former reflects an interest in establishing a philosophy of life because of the failure of familial relationships in providing security, but it does not adequately provide that the person achieve security through such a philosophy before he can endorse the items of the subtest.

An attempt was made to overcome these difficulties in the revision of the subtest. It was decided to avoid concepts that are a distinct part of an established orthodoxy and must be endorsed by anyone accepting the orthodoxy be he mature or immature. Furthermore, emphasis was placed upon the satisfaction, serenity, and inner harmony that characterize the person who has achieved a successful philosophy. Statements of mere intention, belief or orientation were avoided, since endorsement of such a statement does not necessarily indicate that the individual has found security. It has been a point of principle to avoid the specific term "religion" in phrasing items, and to substitute the terms "value," "philosophy," and "purpose," not only to avoid controversy, but also because mature dependent security may be found outside established religious denominations as well as within them. On the other hand, an attempt has been made to avoid the purely intellectual implications of the term "philosophy," and to emphasize instead the function of a philosophy of life in helping the person to face his personal problems.

In summary, the mature dependent security subtest was so designed that to be able to endorse the items the person must have worked out for himself a philosophy of life and a value system and made these his own; he must thereby gain satisfaction, serenity, and inner harmony; his philosophy must give him a sense of belonging in the larger scheme of things by virtue of contribution and participation; his value system must give him a long-range orientation and function as a flexible guide to behaviour; and finally, his philosophy must give him a tolerance of insecurity about matters that necessarily lie far outside his knowledge and control.

In this complex area it was not possible to frame each item to reflect all these aspects of mature dependent security, but each of these aspects was represented by one or more items. Three items were taken over from the first version of the subtest, two of them without change, and three new items were added.

Immature Dependent Security

The prototype of immature dependent security is to be found in the familial area of adjustment. The person is secure because he can count on someone else to look after him, to satisfy his needs, to set his standards, and to protect him from danger and from the consequences of his own actions. In the philosophical area, this function is attributed to some higher power, acting as a parent surrogate.

Both mature and immature dependent security are represented within the framework of Christianity and in other organized religions also. The concept of immature dependent security is embodied in the requirement of a child-like faith in the beneficent omnipotence of God the Father. Mature dependent security is represented in the demand that the individual act maturely, taking moral responsibility for the consequences of his actions, and in the further demand that he achieve a true understanding of the dogma and code, assimilate it and make it quite his own. It was intended that the immature dependent security subtest would emphasize both a child-like faith in being looked after and the fact that this faith was taken over in a child-like way, without question and without working it through. Furthermore, as it is believed that the immaturely dependent person characteristically wants certainty and is intolerant of the insecurity implicit in a flexible value system and in a philosophy that does not provide final answers to all the ultimate questions, items were included which reflected satisfaction with a rigid set of rules to be followed and security in having no unanswered questions.

The first version of the subtest was fairly satisfactory in every respect but one, namely, that it was found to be positively related to the mature dependent security subtest. The fault was believed to lie chiefly with the latter subtest, for the immature dependent security subtest was found to be positively related, as expected, to the immature dependent security subtests of the other tests. But since it was hoped to reduce the overlap between the mature and immature dependent security subtests in the revision of the philosophical test, attention was devoted to revising both. A chief step in revision was to omit reference, directly or by implication, to religious concepts that would have to be accepted by anyone subscribing to an established religion, whether he was secure or insecure, mature or immature. Thus, the revised version avoids reference to God, immortality, and religion as such, and the emphasis remains on the individual's child-like belief that he will be looked after, that all questions will be answered for him, and that his destiny is directed for him.

In summary, immature dependent security in the philosophical area is defined in terms of the following points: the person feels assured that he will be looked after and that he need take no responsibility for his own future; he accepts a dogma and code without taking the responsibility for making it his own by working it through himself, by doubting it, and by trying to understand it; needing certainty, he prefers rules to flexible goals. All of this is successful in giving him contentment and peace of mind.

Three of the items of the revised subtest are new. Three were taken over from the previous version, two of them without change.

Insecurity

As stated before, insecurity arises when the person realizes the limitations of the security resting upon dependence on other people and upon his own competences. Obviously, the person who has no adequate basis for dependent security in intimacies and who lacks confidence in himself will come more readily to an acute recognition of the limitations of human agents than the person who is generally secure in other areas of adjustment. Therefore, it may be expected that insecurity in the philosophical area is in part a generalized insecurity stemming from maladjustment in other areas.

The first version of the subtest portrayed the insecure person as one tending to be confused, futile, frustrated, undecided, disturbed, lonely and guilty. According to expectations, the subtest was found to be positively related, to a highly significant degree, to the insecurity subtests of other tests, and particularly to insecurity in the familial area. On the other hand, many of the items were infrequently endorsed, despite the fact that they seemed to be worded mildly. In revising the subtest the chief emphasis was upon rewording old items and selecting new items so that more frequent endorsement might be obtained. It was anticipated that this effort might not be wholly successful, since it seems likely that only a limited number of young adults have faced an insecurity in other areas of adjustment critical enough to lead them to realize a need for a philosophy of life and to appreciate their own insecurity in this area.

The new selection of items may be classified as reflecting the following indications of insecurity: (a) feelings of frustration and helplessness, (b) a feeling that one is surrounded by a hostile world; (c) feelings of futility and purposelessness; (d) feelings of guilt because of having departed from the beliefs taught in the home; (e) feelings of guilt about behaviour; (f) an uneasy preoccupation with the future, death, and the hereafter.

Deputy Agents

The original version of the deputy agents subtest was intended to reflect defences against insecurity in the philosophical area which take the form of belittling the significance and function of religion and values, or of rationalizing why the person had not formulated a philosophy, or of not tolerating any beliefs and values other than his own. The items were infrequently endorsed. There was little internal consistency in the subtest, and the expectations of the rationale were not fulfilled in the correlations of this subtest with other subtests. It was necessary, therefore, to make a fresh start in the revision. The concepts remain similar, but the items themselves are all new.

The three chief mechanisms represented in the new subtest are as follows:

(a) An attempt to escape feelings of isolation and futility by identification with an authoritarian organization or leader. The implication is that this is an escape from feeling responsible for one's own actions and decisions and from working out a value system for oneself. This is a mode of regression which has much in common with the immature dependent solution. (b) The rationalization of the lack of a philosophy, goals and values by a variety of means, such as a hedonistic outlook or emphasis upon the relativity of morals. (c) Intolerance of the beliefs of others (on the assumption that intolerance occurs to the extent that the faith the person has in his own beliefs is shaky).

Item Analysis of the First Revision of the Philosophical Test

Table IV shows the percentages of "true," "false," and "cannot say" answers to each of the items of the test, together with the coefficients of internal consistency.

TABLE IV

ITEM ANALYSIS OF PHILOSOPHICAL TEST (FIRST REVISION) SHOWING COEFFICIENTS
OF INTERNAL CONSISTENCY AND PERCENTAGES OF "TRUE," "FALSE," AND "CANNOT
SAY" ANSWERS

Subtest	Item	r	% "True"	% "False"	% "Cannot say"
Mature	1	.39	34.3	42.3	23.4
Dependent	6	.65	54.3	25.7	20.0
Security	11	.53	36.0	29.1	34.9
	16	.48	37.1	40.6	22.3
	17	.50	43.4	40.0	16.6
	36	.36	51.5	32.6	16.0
Immature	3	.70	30.3	57.1	12.6
Dependent	10	.36	17.1	65.7	17.1
Security	15	.68	20.6	64.6	14.9
	21	.36	5.7	81.7	12.6
	23	.56	25.7	65.7	8.6
	27	.55	13.1	77.7	9.2
Deputy	4	.41	9.7	79.4	10.9
Agents	8	.32	16.0	73.1	10.9
	9	.13	10.3	73.1	16.6
	12	.48	16.6	69.1	14.3
	20	.31	22.3	56.0	21.7
	22	.34	37.7	50.3	12.0
	25	.37	22.3	57.1	20.6
	26	.21	4.6	85.7	9.7
	30	.11	6.9	85.1	8.0
	32	.55	26.9	58.3	14.9
	33	.23	26.3	60.6	13.1
	35	.61	9.7	85.2	5.1
Insecurity	2	.29	9.7	77.1	13.2
	5	.33	18.9	65.1	16.0
	7	.48	12.6	76.0	11.4
	13	.42	56.6	30.9	12.6
	14	.26	5.7	86.9	7.4
	18	.37	14.9	78.3	6.8
	19	.36	17.1	70.9	12.0
	24	.39	26.9	60.6	12.6
	28	.47	22.3	70.9	6.8
	29	.53	37.1	54.3	8.6
	31	.42	6.3	85.7	8.0
	34	.48	4.6	90.8	4.6

The mature dependent security subtest is the only one that is wholly satisfactory in terms of the criterion of percentage endorsement of the "true" answers. Item 21 should be discarded from the immature dependent security subtest because it is too infrequently endorsed. Items 2, 14, 31, and 34 of the insecurity subtest fail to meet the criterion, as do items 4, 26, 30 and 35 of the deputy agents subtest. Despite these losses the new version is more satisfactory than the old with respect to the criterion of percentage endorsements.

The criterion of internal consistency is met by all of the items of the mature and immature dependent security subtests and by all but items 2 and 14 of the insecurity subtest, both of which also failed to meet the 10 per cent criterion with respect to endorsements. The eight satisfactory items of the insecurity subtest cover all the points listed on page 50 except for feelings of futility and purposelessness. The deputy agents subtest was least successful, with items 9, 26, 30 and 33 falling short of the criterion of internal consistency; two of them also failed to meet the 10 per cent criterion. Altogether, six items remain, and these cover the three mechanisms described on page 50.

VII RELIABILITY OF THE SUBTESTS

Using Hoyt's method (7) for estimating the reliability of a test on the basis of its internal consistency, reliability coefficients were calculated for each of the subtests. (See Table V.) In this calculation all items were included, not just those which had met the criteria set up in the item analysis. On the whole, the reliability coefficients are remarkably high, considering that ten of the subtests are composed

TABLE V

RELIABILITY COEFFICIENTS OF THE SUBTESTS OF THE FOUR TESTS OF SECURITY

Subtest	Familial test	Extra-Familial test	Avoca-tional test	Philo-sophical test	Combined tests
Independent Security	.900	.600	.433	. . .	.657
Mature Dependent Security	. . .	.546	.766	.590	.737
Immature Dependent Security	.655	.613	.549	.661	.733
Deputy Agents	.398	.510	.741	.601	.791
Insecurity	.672	.723	.656	.597	.829

of only six items each. The subtests with the most satisfactory reliability are: independent security in the familial test, mature dependent security and deputy agents in the avocational test, and insecurity in the extra-familial test, with coefficients of .900, .766, .741 and .723 respectively.

There are only two subtests with reliability coefficients below .500, a level which is the usual requirement for subtests of group intelligence tests. These two are the deputy agents subtest of the familial test and the independent security subtest of the avocational test. Both of these subtests presented unexpected differences between the Canadian samples upon which the earlier versions had been tried out and the English sample upon which the present statistics are based. In both instances a large proportion of the items failed to meet the criteria for item retention. It will be recalled that, in the case of the independent security subtest of the avocational test, all items were frequently endorsed by the English sample and three items were too frequently endorsed to be acceptable; yet the items had been infrequently endorsed by a comparable Canadian sample. In the case of the deputy agents subtest of the familial test, two of the items which had failed to meet a satisfactory degree of internal consistency with the English sample were items that had had the highest coefficients of internal consistency in the case of the Canadian sample. It may well be, therefore, that even these two subtests would prove to be reliable when used with a Canadian population.

The standard errors of the measures given by all subtests are shown in Table VI. From the standard error it is possible to estimate how far from the obtained score (the number of "true" answers to the items of the subtest in question) of the individual his "true" score is likely

TABLE VI

STANDARD ERRORS OF THE MEASURES GIVEN BY THE SUBTESTS OF THE FOUR SECURITY TESTS

Subtest	Familial test	Extra-Familial test	Avoca-tional test	Philo-sophical test	Combined tests
Independent Security	.67	.94	.86	...	1.73
Mature Dependent Security	...	.93	.88	.99	1.82
Immature Dependent Security	.87	.94	.96	.74	2.02
Deputy Agents	1.45	1.29	1.20	1.15	2.71
Insecurity	1.15	1.35	1.18	1.16	2.53

to lie. The chances are 95 in 100 that his true score will fall within the range of twice the standard error above or below the obtained score. For example, one could be reasonably sure that the "true" score of an individual on the independent security subtest of the familial test would be not more than 1.34 points higher or lower than his obtained score. Since the range of obtained scores must fall within the range of 0 to 6, however, it is obvious that this represents a substantial degree of error, even for this subtest which has the smallest standard error. For the mature dependent security subtest of the philosophical test one could not reasonably rely upon the scores within two points (to be precise, 1.98). For the deputy agents and insecurity subtests which are composed of twelve items each, the range of reasonable confidence is from 2.3 points in the case of the insecurity subtest of the familial test to 2.9 points in the case of the deputy agents subtest of the same test. This means that only scores at the extremes of the possible range could be relied upon to indicate even a tendency toward either security or insecurity.

The justification for using a subtest containing a small number of items and for accepting a relatively low reliability coefficient as satisfactory is that it is to be combined with other subtests measuring the same variable. It is expected that the larger number of items in the combination of subtests will result in a satisfactory degree of reliability.

There are two possibilities open when it comes to combining the subtests of the four tests together. One possibility is to construct some composite score for each test that gives positive and negative weights to each of the subtest scores in accordance with an *a priori* judgment of the contribution each score makes either to the total security of the individual or to his over-all mental health. This alternative was chosen by Grapko (6), who developed a "mental health quotient" derived from another parallel revision of the security tests. The second possibility is to combine the four tests of the battery together by combining comparable subtests, assuming equal weight for all component items. This would yield five scores: independent security, mature dependent security, immature dependent security, deputy agents and insecurity. In the present study this alternative is chosen.

In Table V the reliability coefficients of the combined subtests are shown. These all reach a reasonably satisfactory level. The highest coefficients are found with the insecurity and deputy agents subtests, .829 and .791 respectively. These two combined subtests have 48 items each. The immature dependent security subtest with 24 items has a coefficient of .733. The independent security and mature dependent security subtests have 18 items each, and therefore could be expected to have somewhat lower coefficients. The coefficient of the mature dependent security subtest is actually .737, about the same as that of the immature dependent security subtest. The fact that the coefficient of the independent security subtest is as low as .637 is probably due to the influence of the independent security subtest of the avocational test which has low reliability.

With the possible range of scores extended in this manner, the battery of tests could be used to give reasonably reliable measures for the individual. Working from the standard errors shown in Table VI, the following statements may be deduced. In the case of the insecurity subtest, for which the actual range of scores was 0 to 35, there are 95 chances in 100 that an individual's "true" score is within 5.06 points of his obtained score. This does not make possible fine differentiations between individuals, but permits a reliable coarse classification. The same is true of the deputy agents, immature dependent security and mature dependent security scores. For the deputy agents subtest with an obtained range of scores between 0 and 33, there are 95 chances in 100 that the individual's "true" score is within 5.42 points of his obtained score. For the immature dependent security subtest with an obtained range of 0 to 20, there are 95 chances in 100 that his "true" score is within 4.04 points of his obtained score. For the mature dependent security subtest, with both a possible and an obtained range of 0 to 18, there are 95 chances in 100 that the individual's "true" score is within 3.64 points of his obtained score. The independent security subtest is less satisfactory. The obtained range was from 5 to 18 points, and there are 95 chances in 100 that the individual's "true" score is within 3.46 points of his obtained score.

VIII SCORING

For the purposes of the analysis of reliability it was necessary to ignore all but the "true" answers and to give each of these equal weight. On this basis, the "score" for each subtest is a simple total of the "true" answers.

The frequency distributions obtained when the subtests are scored in this way are shown in Tables VII, VIII, IX and X. From inspection it may be seen that the distributions of the independent security and deputy agents subtests of the familial test and the mature dependent security subtest of the extra-familial test approximate a normal distribution. In addition, the independent security subtest of the extra-familial test and the mature dependent security subtest of the philosophical test have distributions close enough to normal to be considered as such. The other subtests are all skewed to a greater or less

TABLE VII

Frequency Distribution of "True" Answers for the Subtests of the Familial Test

Number of "True" Answers	Independent Security	Immature Dependent Security	Deputy Agents	Insecurity
12	..	..	0	0
11	..	..	0	0
10	..	..	0	0
9	..	..	3	1
8	..	..	10	1
7	..	..	18	5
6	12	5	29	9
5	26	6	35	8
4	28	24	31	8
3	39	22	23	21
2	35	29	17	26
1	30	46	6	53
0	5	43	3	43
Total	175	175	175	175

TABLE VIII

FREQUENCY DISTRIBUTIONS OF "TRUE" ANSWERS FOR THE SUBTESTS OF THE EXTRA-
FAMILIAL TEST

Number of "True" Answers	Frequencies in Subtests				
	Independent Security	Mature Dependent Security	Immature Dependent Security	Deputy Agents	Insecurity
12	..	..	..	0	0
11	..	..	..	0	0
10	..	..	..	1	4
9	..	..	..	0	8
8	..	..	..	2	11
7	..	..	..	6	9
6	11	8	6	12	18
5	35	29	17	14	22
4	30	53	30	22	23
3	31	42	35	27	26
2	39	27	30	44	19
1	21	10	34	35	16
0	8	6	23	12	19
Total	175	175	175	175	175

TABLE IX

FREQUENCY DISTRIBUTIONS OF "TRUE" ANSWERS FOR THE SUBTESTS OF THE
AVOCATIONAL TEST

Number of "True" Answers	Frequencies in Subtests				
	Independent Security	Mature Dependent Security	Immature Dependent Security	Deputy Agents	Insecurity
12	..	..	..	0	0
11	..	..	..	0	0
10	..	..	..	1	0
9	..	..	..	2	2
8	..	..	..	4	1
7	..	..	..	7	3
6	61	18	8	5	6
5	43	24	6	16	18
4	40	16	19	21	15
3	21	29	28	27	26
2	8	26	51	40	25
1	2	29	36	24	47
0	0	33	27	28	32
Total	175	175	175	175	175

TABLE X

FREQUENCY DISTRIBUTIONS OF "TRUE" ANSWERS FOR THE SUBTESTS OF THE
PHILOSOPHICAL TEST

Number of "True" Answers	Mature Dependent Security	Frequencies in Subtests Immature Dependent Security	Deputy Agents	Insecurity
12	..	..	0	0
11	..	..	1	0
10	..	..	0	2
9	..	..	0	0
8	..	..	1	2
7	..	..	6	2
6	8	0	3	4
5	22	6	7	11
4	20	10	12	17
3	36	14	23	34
2	36	21	50	29
1	31	43	35	51
0	22	81	37	23
Total	175	175	175	175

extent. The greatest skews are found in the immature dependent
security subtest of the philosophical test and the independent security
subtest of the avocational test. The latter is the only subtest yielding
a negative skew, and this may be accounted for by the fact that the
items were too frequently endorsed. In the remaining tests the skews
are not excessive and are all positive. In the case of the mature
dependent security subtest of the avocational test the positive skew
means that the desirable (secure) extreme is less frequently represented than the undesirable (insecure) extreme. All other instances
of positive skew have the reverse implication, with the desirable
extreme being more frequently represented. Thus, in the frequency
distributions of the insecurity subtests, all of which were somewhat
skewed, the cases bulk towards the end of the continuum indicating
absence of insecurity. The distributions of all the deputy agents subtests, except the one in the familial test, are similarly skewed, so that
the cases bulk towards the end of the continuum indicating relative
absence of defence mechanisms. The distributions of all of the immature dependent security subtests are more or less skewed, so that
most cases fall towards the end of the continuum indicating relative
absence of immature dependent security.

TABLE XI

DISTRIBUTION OF "CANNOT SAY" ANSWERS TO ITEMS OF THE FAMILIAL TEST WHEN
SUBJECTS ARE DIVIDED INTO QUINTILES ON THE BASIS OF "TRUE" ANSWERS

| Subtest | Item | Frequency of "cannot say" answers | | | | | | Highest quintiles |
		Q5	Q4	Q3	Q2	Q1	Total	
Independent	1	0	4	3	4	6	17	1
Security	2	1	5	5	9	8	28	2
	6	1	6	5	8	17	37	1
	15	3	6	4	5	5	23	4–1
	20	0	1	0	4	7	12	1
	36	1	6	6	5	10	28	1
Immature	3	7	5	6	3	1	22	5
Dependent	7	2	10	8	4	3	27	4
Security	16	0	6	9	7	6	28	3
	19	3	7	0	5	0	15	4
	25	1	9	10	4	0	24	3
	26	2	5	2	4	3	16	4
Deputy	5	2	2	1	2	4	11	1
Agents	9	2	4	1	2	5	14	1
	10	3	4	3	4	2	16	4–2
	13	2	4	2	1	4	13	4–1
	14	1	1	0	4	4	10	2–1
	21	1	1	1	4	4	11	2–1
	22	3	4	1	4	2	14	4–2
	28	2	6	6	6	4	24	4–2
	29	3	5	5	3	3	19	4–3
	33	2	1	5	2	6	16	3–1
	34	4	4	6	10	6	30	2
	35	6	6	8	4	3	27	3
Insecurity	4	0	3	1	3	0	7	4–2
	8	1	3	2	4	2	12	2
	11	4	4	5	6	0	19	2
	12	2	1	2	0	2	7	5–1
	17	3	0	3	2	0	8	5–3
	18	3	2	4	3	1	13	3
	23	0	2	6	3	0	11	3
	24	2	2	6	2	3	15	3
	27	7	3	2	3	0	15	5
	30	7	0	3	1	1	12	5
	31	6	2	3	1	0	12	5
	32	2	2	2	0	0	6	5–3

TABLE XII

Subtest	Item	Frequency of "cannot say" answers						Highest quintiles
		Q5	Q4	Q3	Q2	Q1	Total	
Independent	2	3	6	7	12	7	35	2
Security	8	0	1	0	7	11	19	1
	17	2	0	3	7	9	21	1
	24	2	1	4	12	5	24	2
	34	2	8	9	7	5	31	3
	36	3	7	7	13	11	41	2
Mature	1	6	13	6	8	2	35	4
Dependent	9	3	9	9	8	5	34	4–3
Security	16	0	0	0	1	2	3	1
	25	1	1	4	8	6	20	2
	35	0	4	7	2	3	16	3
	39	0	3	1	3	4	11	1
Immature	3	4	6	6	12	6	34	2
Dependent	4	11	5	7	7	5	35	5
Security	10	1	3	8	4	2	18	3
	18	1	8	11	7	3	30	3
	19	4	7	10	8	2	31	3
	26	0	3	2	4	6	15	1
Deputy	6	2	2	10	6	4	24	3
Agents	7	9	12	9	12	5	47	4–2
	13	2	7	6	4	2	21	4
	14	1	2	4	2	1	10	3
	15	1	6	8	6	1	22	3
	20	5	4	1	3	1	14	5
	21	2	4	3	3	3	15	4
	29	2	3	3	6	7	21	1
	30	2	7	2	2	2	15	4
	31	1	5	4	2	2	14	4
	32	4	6	4	3	5	22	5
	33	3	3	3	2	2	13	5–3
Insecurity	5	0	1	5	5	6	17	1
	11	1	4	5	5	4	19	3–2
	12	4	3	6	2	1	16	3
	22	4	0	1	1	1	7	5
	23	2	3	1	3	0	9	4–2
	27	5	3	9	5	4	26	3
	28	2	4	8	3	2	19	3
	37	3	4	5	3	2	17	3
	38	2	3	6	0	4	15	3
	40	4	1	6	4	4	19	3
	41	5	2	2	1	1	11	5
	42	7	6	3	2	2	20	5

TABLE XIII

DISTRIBUTION OF "CANNOT SAY" ANSWERS TO ITEMS OF THE AVOCATIONAL TEST WHEN SUBJECTS ARE DIVIDED INTO QUINTILES ON THE BASIS OF "TRUE" ANSWERS

| Subtest | Item | Frequency of "cannot say" answers | | | | | | Highest quintiles |
		Q5	Q4	Q3	Q2	Q1	Total	
Independent	2	0	2	1	5	10	18	1
Security	11	0	4	3	1	6	14	1
	16	0	1	1	2	7	11	1
	17	0	0	2	5	10	17	1
	24	0	1	2	4	5	12	1
	29	0	1	4	8	2	15	2
Mature	1	1	5	4	1	3	14	4
Dependent	12	5	6	5	3	3	22	4
Security	18	0	5	5	1	3	14	4–3
	19	4	9	6	6	4	29	4
	34	1	2	7	4	5	19	3
	39	2	11	8	3	2	26	4
Immature	3	2	5	4	6	7	24	1
Dependent	13	1	10	6	7	2	26	4
Security	15	2	9	8	5	5	29	4
	25	4	3	5	8	2	22	2
	26	3	14	6	9	8	40	4
	30	3	4	2	7	3	19	2
Deputy	6	2	8	8	4	7	29	4–3
Agents	7	1	5	5	5	2	18	4–2
	8	3	2	9	0	0	14	3
	20	2	8	7	2	3	22	4
	21	0	5	4	2	3	14	4
	27	2	5	6	2	5	20	3
	28	4	5	5	0	2	16	4–3
	32	2	2	5	5	4	18	3–2
	33	2	3	5	0	1	11	3
	37	3	4	1	1	1	10	4
	38	3	3	4	2	0	12	3
	41	2	5	5	2	1	15	4–3
Insecurity	4	3	2	0	0	0	5	5
	5	2	1	4	1	2	10	3
	9	2	1	4	0	3	10	3
	10	2	3	4	0	1	10	3
	14	4	1	3	0	2	10	5
	22	5	2	1	1	4	13	5
	23	2	1	3	0	1	7	3
	31	2	1	2	0	1	6	5–3
	35	6	2	3	0	1	12	5
	36	1	0	4	1	0	6	3
	40	3	0	2	0	1	6	5
	42	2	0	1	0	1	4	5

TABLE XIV

DISTRIBUTION OF "CANNOT SAY" ANSWERS TO ITEMS OF THE PHILOSOPHICAL TEST
WHEN SUBJECTS ARE DIVIDED INTO QUINTILES ON THE BASIS OF "TRUE" ANSWERS

Subtest	Item	Frequency of "cannot say" answers						Highest quintiles
		Q5	Q4	Q3	Q2	Q1	Total	
Mature	1	3	10	8	11	9	41	2
Dependent	6	1	4	5	13	12	35	2
Security	11	5	13	16	13	14	61	3
	16	2	8	10	10	9	39	3-2
	17	2	7	8	9	3	29	2
	36	3	6	5	8	6	28	2
Immature	3	2	11	6	3	0	22	4
Dependent	10	9	6	8	7	0	30	5
Security	15	3	10	7	6	0	26	4
	21	6	6	6	4	0	22	5-3
	23	0	5	6	4	0	15	3
	27	3	8	4	1	0	16	4
Deputy	4	7	7	1	2	2	19	5-4
Agents	8	5	3	4	3	4	19	5
	9	10	9	2	5	3	29	5
	12	4	10	1	4	6	25	4
	20	8	7	8	9	6	38	2
	22	5	6	0	3	7	21	1
	25	2	8	9	9	8	36	3-2
	26	5	7	0	2	3	17	4
	30	6	4	2	1	1	14	5
	32	1	10	4	4	7	26	4
	33	3	6	3	4	7	23	1
	35	3	4	0	1	1	9	4
Insecurity	2	4	6	8	4	1	23	3
	5	6	8	3	4	7	28	4
	7	7	4	4	3	2	20	5
	13	3	3	6	4	6	22	3-1
	14	5	2	2	3	1	13	5
	18	2	5	3	2	0	12	4
	19	6	4	1	3	4	21	5
	24	7	0	5	6	4	22	5
	28	3	3	3	2	1	12	5-3
	29	4	2	5	3	1	15	3
	31	5	1	4	2	2	14	5
	34	3	2	2	0	1	8	5

It was decided to explore the desirability of modifying the subtest scores by including "cannot say" answers as well as "true" answers. It was our impression that "cannot say" answers might be considered a weak positive reply, and that they tended to be associated with "true" rather than "false" answers within a given subtest. If this proved to be so, to include "cannot say" answers in determining the scores would serve to reduce the skew in all positively skewed distributions.

The method of exploration adopted was to divide the population into quintiles on the basis of the number of items answered "true" and to count the number of "cannot say" replies given for each item by each quintile. The results are shown in Tables XI, XII, XIII and XIV. It may be seen that the "cannot say" answers were more frequent in the higher quintiles in the case of ten subtests: the immature dependent security and insecurity subtests of the familial test; the deputy agents and insecurity subtests of the extra-familial test; the mature dependent security, deputy agents and insecurity subtests of the avocational test; and the immature dependent security, deputy agents and insecurity subtests of the philosophical test. With these subtests, the subjects who gave more "true" answers tended to give more "cannot say" answers than the subjects who gave fewer "true" answers. For these subtests, therefore, weighted scores were calculated, assigning each "cannot say" answer a weight of one-half, and each "true" answer a weight of one. The distributions were not markedly altered by this change, and hence are not shown here, but the slight changes which did result were all in the direction of reducing the degree of skew. In the remaining subtests the "true" answers were given a weight of one, and the "cannot say" and "false" answers each a weight of zero.

IX INTERRELATIONSHIPS BETWEEN SUBTEST SCORES

As a check on the validity of the subtests an examination was made of the interrelationships between the subtest scores to ascertain the extent to which the obtained relationships were consistent with expectations derived from the underlying rationale. To the extent to which a given subtest fails to be related as expected to other subtests it may be judged to be invalid, since it is not measuring what it was intended to measure. This check of validity seems an essential first step in validation research, but it is not intended as a substitute for checking each subtest against some appropriate criterion outside the tests themselves, difficult as it would be to set up such criteria. Within the scope of the present study, however, an examination of inter-correlations between subtests was the only feasible check on validity.

According to the rationale, the following relationships are to be expected:

(1) A substantial positive relationship between those subtests which measure the same mode of adjustment but in different tests, and a high positive relationship between each subtest and the "combined subtest total" to which it contributes. Thus, it is expected that each independent security subtest will be positively related to each of the other two independent security subtests and to the independent security total. Similarly, it is expected that each mature dependent security subtest will be positively related to each of the other mature dependent security subtests and to the mature dependent security total.

(2) For the independent security subtests and total the following pattern of inter-correlations is expected: a positive correlation with all mature dependent security subtests, zero correlations with immature dependent security and deputy agents subtests, and low negative correlations with insecurity subtests. The positive correlation with the mature dependent security subtests is to be expected since both sets of subtests are intended to reflect both security and a mature mode of adjustment. The negative correlation with the insecurity subtests is

expected to be low rather than high, since independent security is intended to imply tolerance for insecurity, and hence it is not expected that independently secure people will be entirely lacking in insecure feelings. A zero rather than a negative correlation with immature dependent security is expected because of two conflicting trends. The fact that one subtest reflects independence and the other dependence would make for a negative correlation, but the fact that both subtests reflect security would make for a positive correlation, and the resultant of these two tendencies should be a correlation approximating zero. An exception is expected in the case of the familial test, which was constructed with the intention of producing a negative correlation between independent security and immature dependent security. The greatest difficulty was in clarifying the expectations with respect to the relationship between independent security and deputy agents subtests. Since it was expected that deputy agents should be positively related to insecurity, and that insecurity should be negatively related to independent security, it might also be expected that deputy agents would be negatively related to independent security. On the other hand, a moderate and successful use of defence mechanisms might be expected to supplement independent security. On the whole, it was decided that a zero relationship would be congruent with the rationale, although a low negative relationship would not be taken as an indication of invalidity.

(3) For the mature dependent security subtests and total the following pattern is expected: a positive correlation with both independent security and immature dependent security subtests, a zero correlation with deputy agents subtests, and a negative correlation with insecurity subtests. Positive correlations are expected between mature dependent security and both independent and immature dependent security since all are secure modes of adjustment, although the contrasts between independence and dependence on the one hand and between mature and immature on the other hand would tend to keep the correlations low. The zero correlation with deputy agents is expected on the same basis as it is expected in the case of independent security and deputy agents.

(4) For the immature dependent security subtests and total the following pattern is expected: a zero correlation with independent security, a positive correlation with mature dependent security, both of which have already been discussed, and a low positive correlation with both deputy agents and insecurity. The low positive correlation with insecurity is expected on the grounds that immature dependent

security in the adult is a brittle and vulnerable adjustment, constantly threatening to break down into insecurity. The low positive correlation with deputy agents is expected because in the adult immature dependent security is somewhat regressive in nature and thus constitutes a defence mechanism in itself.

(5) For the insecurity subtests the expectations are as follows: low negative correlations with independent and mature dependent security, a low positive correlation with immature dependent security and a substantial positive correlation with deputy agents. This latter expectation rests on the view that the presence of defence mechanisms is no indication that they are successful in defending against the insecurity that gave rise to their use. On the contrary, insecurity is likely to recur because the defences provide no constructive solution to the original problem from which insecurity arose, and the mechanisms themselves may interfere with adjustment and occasion further insecurity.

(6) For the deputy agents subtests the expectations have already been stated: zero correlation with independent and mature dependent security, a low positive correlation with immature dependent security and a substantial positive correlation with insecurity.

A word should be added concerning intra-test correlations as contrasted with inter-test correlations. To indicate validity in terms of congruence with the expectations from the rationale, the expectations should be met more closely in inter-correlations among subtests of the same test than in correlations with subtests of other tests.

Product-moment correlations were calculated for each pair of subtests and for each subtest with each total. Correlations with the totals were included as an additional check. If the correlation between a given pair of subtests proves to be out of line with expectations, it is not clear which of the two subtests is at fault. The correlation of each with the total to which the other contributes provides one way of ascertaining which of the subtests is at fault, and the other inter-correlations may be expected to help in clarifying the issue. The inter-test and intra-test correlations are shown in Table XV. It may be noted that, with 175 subjects, the following levels of significance hold: a correlation coefficient of .148 is significant at the 5 per cent level, one of .176 is significant at the 2 per cent level, and one of .195 or higher is significant at the 1 per cent level. All coefficients lower than .148 are taken as not significantly exceeding zero.

In discussing these inter-correlations it is proposed to consider each of the five types of subtest in turn, beginning with the insecurity

TABLE XV

INTER-TEST AND INTRA-TEST CORRELATIONS OF THE SUBTESTS OF FOUR SECURITY TESTS

Test	Subtest	Independent Security				Mature Dependent Security				Immature Dependent Security				
		Familial	Extra-Familial	Avo-cational	Total	Extra-Familial	Avo-cational	Philo-sophical	Total	Familial	Extra-Familial	Avo-cational	Philo-sophical	Total
Independent Security	Familial	....	.353**	.092	.715**	.091	-.112	.162*	.016	-.215**	-.119	.171*	-.135	-.128
	Extra-Familial	.353**	....	.200**	.775**	.452**	.129	.370**	.397**	.065	.058	.208**	.054	.153*
	Avocational	.092	.200**	....	.555**	.172*	.225**	.229**	.267**	.029	.143	.032	-.030	.086
	Total	.715**	.775**	.555**	....	.353**	.093	.380**	.323**	-.067	.024	.203**	-.059	-.042
Mature Dependent Security	Extra-Familial	.091	.452**	.172*	.353**	....	.233**	.344**	.650**	.080	.304**	.183*	.160*	.304**
	Avocational	-.112	.129	.225**	.093	.233**	....	.249**	.746**	.232**	.394**	.049	.278**	.385**
	Philosophical	.162*	.370**	.229**	.380**	.344**	.249**	....	.690**	.219**	.283**	-.049	.220**	.269**
	Total	.016	.397**	.267**	.323**	.650**	.746**	.690**	....	.248**	.449**	.085	.319**	.449**
Immature Dependent Security	Familial	-.215**	.065	.029	-.067	.080	.232**	.219**	.248**	....	.288**	.073	.314**	.692**
	Extra-Familial	-.119	.058	.143	.024	.304**	.394**	.283**	.449**	.288**	....	.042	.287**	.677**
	Avocational	.171*	.208**	.032	.203**	.183*	.049	-.049	.085	.073	.042	....	-.088	.421**
	Philosophical	-.135	.054	-.030	-.059	.160*	.278**	.220**	.319**	.314**	.287**	-.088	....	.585**
	Total	-.128	.153*	.086	-.042	.304**	.385**	.269**	.449**	.692**	.677**	.421**	.585**	....
Deputy Agents	Familial	-.139	-.013	.380**	-.028	.091	.198**	.142	.208**	.333**	.367**	-.008	.198**	.353**
	Extra-Familial	.039	.041	-.046	.006	-.181*	.171*	.083	.044	.266**	.123	.129	.093	.238**
	Avocational	.033	.037	-.035	.016	-.067	.280**	.080	.151*	.100	.190*	-.005	.197**	.173*
	Philosophical	.057	.109	-.144	.018	.045	.205**	.054	.183*	.103	.137	.206**	.155*	.243**
	Total	-.009	.048	-.018	.001	-.034	.282**	.128	.195**	.264**	.248**	.112	.199**	.321**
Insecurity	Familial	-.228**	-.132	-.082	-.223**	-.078	.088	-.031	.024	.123	.288**	.051	.109	.225**
	Extra-Familial	-.084	-.379**	-.054	-.259**	-.253**	.079	-.001	-.058	-.239**	.016	.016	.076	.252**
	Avocational	-.014	-.101	-.202**	-.147	-.204**	-.018	-.060	-.106	.092	.038	.165*	-.048	.095
	Philosophical	-.125	-.288**	-.108	-.255**	-.206**	.145	-.180*	-.055	.092	.324**	.111	.099	.269**
	Total	-.128	-.305**	-.139	-.282**	-.237**	.108	-.076	-.053	.174*	.313**	.123	.064	.275**

TABLE XV—continued

		Deputy Agents					Insecurity				
		Familial	Extra-Familial	Avocational	Philosophical	Total	Familial	Extra-Familial	Avocational	Philosophical	Total
Independent Security	Familial	−.139	.039	.033	.057	−.009	−.228**	−.084	−.014	−.125	−.128
	Extra-Familial	−.013	.041	.037	.109	.048	−.132	−.379**	−.101	−.288**	−.305**
	Avocational	.380**	−.046	−.035	−.144	−.018	−.082	−.054	−.202**	−.108	−.139
	Total	−.028	.006	.016	.018	.001	−.223**	−.259**	−.147	−.255**	−.285**
Mature Security	Extra-Familial	.091	−.181*	−.067	.045	−.034	−.078	−.253**	−.204**	−.206**	−.237**
	Avocational	.198**	.171*	.280**	.205**	.282**	−.088	.079	−.018	.145	.108
	Philosophical	.142	.083	.080	.054	.128	−.031	−.001	−.060	−.180*	−.076
	Total	.208**	.044	.151*	.183*	.195**	.024	−.058	−.106	−.055	−.053
Immature Security	Familial	.333**	.266**	.100	.103	.264**	.123	.239**	.092	.092	.174*
	Extra-Familial	.367**	.123	.190*	.137	.248**	.288**	.293**	.038	.324**	.313**
	Avocational	−.008	.129	−.005	.206**	.112	.051	.016	.165*	.111	.123
	Philosophical	.198**	.093	.197**	.155*	.199**	.109	.076	−.048	.099	.064
	Total	.353**	.238**	.173*	.243**	.321**	.225**	.252**	.095	.269**	.275**
Deputy Agents	Familial		.375**	.294**	.193*	.607**	.334**	.278**	.179*	.299**	.342**
	Extra-Familial	.375**		.540**	.480**	.800**	.410**	.403**	.427**	.362**	.515**
	Avocational	.294**	.540**		.479**	.783**	.344**	.313**	.495**	.387**	.482**
	Philosophical	.193*	.480**	.479**		.712**	.344**	.219**	.430**	.317**	.416**
	Total	.607**	.800**	.783**	.712**		.476**	.410**	.502**	.434**	.579**
Insecurity	Familial	.334**	.410**	.344**	.344**	.476**		.457**	.467**	.505**	.749**
	Extra-Familial	.278**	.403**	.313**	.219**	.410**	.457**		.431**	.489**	.791**
	Avocational	.179*	.427**	.495**	.430**	.502**	.467**	.431**		.528**	.757**
	Philosophical	.299**	.362**	.387**	.317**	.434**	.505**	.489**	.528**		.773**
	Total	.342**	.515**	.482**	.416**	.579**	.749**	.791**	.757**	.773**	....

** r is significant at 1% level.
* r is significant at 5% level.

subtests for which the inter-correlations are most closely in line with expectations.

Insecurity

The first expectation, namely, that there will be a substantial positive correlation between those subtests which measure the same mode of adjustment but in different areas, is best met in the case of the insecurity subtests. All correlations are positive and substantial, and all of the insecurity subtests are highly correlated with the insecurity total. The expectation that the insecurity subtests will be positively correlated with the deputy agents subtests is also met. All coefficients are positive and significant, and nearly all are moderate to substantial rather than low.

The correlations with the independent, mature dependent, and immature dependent security subtests also tend to meet expectations from the rationale, but here the trends are not entirely as predicted. The insecurity subtest of the familial test meets expectations in the case of intra-test correlations, with a significant negative correlation with the independent security subtest in the familial test, and a low positive correlation with the immature dependent security subtest, although the latter falls below the 5 per cent level of significance. In the case of correlations with subtests of other tests the following expectations are met: there is a significant negative correlation with the independent security total and a significant positive correlation with the immature dependent security total, although the correlations with the component subtests are below the level of significance. The correlations with the mature dependent security subtests and total are consistently zero rather than negative, but this finding does not seem to be a sufficiently important departure from expectations to throw doubt on the validity of the insecurity subtest of the familial test.

The insecurity subtest of the extra-familial test meets all expectations with respect to intra-test relationships, with significant negative correlations with the independent and mature dependent security subtests of the extra-familial test and a significant positive correlation with the immature dependent security subtest. The inter-test correlations follow the same pattern but are less consistent in meeting expectations. There is a significant negative correlation with the independent security total, but not with the component subtests. Similarly, there is a significant positive correlation with the immature dependent security total and with that subtest in the familial test, but not with the subtests of the avocational and philosophical tests. As in the case of the insecurity subtest of the familial test, there is a zero relationship with the mature dependent security total and component subtests, rather than the low negative correlation that was expected—and obtained—in the case of intra-test correlation.

The insecurity subtest of the avocational test meets expectations fairly well with respect to intra-test correlations. There is a significant negative correlation with the independent security subtest and a significant positive correlation with the immature dependent security subtest, but there is a zero instead of the expected negative correlation with the mature dependent security subtest. With respect to inter-test correlations, expectations are not clearly met, although there are no striking discrepancies. The correlation with the independent security total is negative as expected, but just below the level of statistical significance. The correlations with the mature dependent and immature dependent security totals are zero rather than the low negative and low positive expected, and the same holds for correlations with five of the subtests contributing to the totals, although in the case of two subtests the correlations are in the expected direction.

The insecurity subtest of the philosophical test has a significant negative correlation with the mature dependent security subtest of the philosophical test, as expected, but the expected positive correlation with the immature dependent security subtest does not emerge. This finding will be discussed later in connection with the latter subtest. With respect to inter-test correlations, the findings tend to be in accordance with expectations. There is a significant negative correlation with the independent security total and with the independent security subtest of the extra-familial test, although the correlations with the other two independent security subtests fall short of significance. There is a significant negative correlation with the mature dependent security subtest of the extra-familial subtest, as expected, but this does not hold for the mature dependent security subtest of the avocational test (which, as will be pointed out later, emerges as an invalid subtest) or for the total. The expected low positive correlation with immature dependent security is found in the case of that subtest of the extra-familial test and the immature dependent security total.

On the whole, the insecurity subtests meet expectations derived from the rationale very well indeed. In the few instances where there is a departure from expectations we are inclined to attribute the fault to the subtests other than those measuring insecurity. In any event, all of these departures are minor ones representing a distinction between insignificant and low correlations.

Independent Security

The independent security subtests are not as successful as the insecurity subtests in meeting the first expectation that subtests measuring the same mode of adjustment in different areas should be correlated with each other substantially and positively. The independent security subtests of the familial and extra-familial tests are but moderately correlated with each other, although both have high correlations with the independent security total to which both contribute. However, the independent security subtest of the avocational test has only a low positive correlation with the corresponding subtest of the extra-familial test and a zero correlation with the corresponding subtest of the familial test. It may be recalled that its reliability coefficient was low, and that the percentage endorsements of several of the component items were too high.

The independent security subtest of the familial test meets the intra-test expectations quite satisfactorily, with a significant negative correlation with the insecurity test of the familial test, a zero correlation with the deputy agents subtest, and a significant negative correlation with the immature dependent security subtest. It meets some of the inter-test correlations satisfactorily. There is the expected zero relationship with all of the deputy agents subtests and with the deputy agents total, and the expected zero relationship with two of the immature dependent security subtests and with the immature dependent security total. There is an unexpected positive correlation with the immature dependent security subtest of the avocational test which, as will be pointed out later, seems attributable to that subtest. It is with respect to the obtained zero correlations with the mature dependent security subtests (except that of the philosophical test), instead of the expected positive correlations and the insignificant size of the expected negative correlations with the insecurity subtests, that the expectations from the rationale are not met. It seems likely that the independent security subtest of the familial test still reflects somewhat too much emphasis upon emancipation, so that some subjects have been able to endorse the items who are more independent than secure. This should be kept in mind when the scores obtained from this subtest in its present form are interpreted.

The independent security subtest of the extra-familial test is more successful in meeting expectations. The intra-test expectations are met very well, with a moderate negative correlation with the insecurity subtest of the extra-familial test, a moderate positive correlation with the mature dependent security subtest, and zero correlations with the immature dependent security and deputy agents subtests. The inter-test correlations follow the same pattern on the whole. There are moderate positive correlations with the mature dependent security total and with the mature dependent security subtest of the philo-sophical test. The insignificant correlation with the mature dependent security subtest of the avocational test is considered a fault of this subtest, which emerges as invalid. There are the expected zero corre-lations with the immature dependent security subtests except in the case of this subtest in the avocational test, and again the fault is attributed to the latter, and the significant positive correlation with the immature dependent security total seems likely to be a function of the contribution made by the avocational subtest to the total. The zero correlations with all of the deputy agents subtests and total are in accordance with expectations. The correlations with the insecurity subtests and total are all negative as expected, although two of the coefficients fall below the level of statistical significance.

Despite the fact that the independent security subtest of the avo-cational test has deficiencies, as previously pointed out, the intra-test correlations meet expectations. There is a positive correlation with the mature dependent security subtest of the avocational test, a negative correlation with the insecurity subtest, and zero correlations with the immature dependent security and deputy agents subtests. The inter-test correlations meet expectations of positive correlations with the mature dependent security subtests and total and zero correlations with the immature dependent security subtests and total. The expected zero correlations are also found in the case of all but one of the deputy agents subtests, but there is an unexpectedly significant positive corre-lation with the deputy agents subtest of the familial test for which there is no obvious explanation.

The independent security total, as might be expected, meets the expectations from the rationale better than the component subtests, except that the independent security subtest of the extra-familial test seems equally satisfactory. In so far as the rationale can provide a criterion of validity, it may be concluded that the independent security total offers a valid measure of independent security, and that the in-dependent security subtest of the extra-familial test approaches the total in degree of validity. The independent security subtest of the familial test needs to be interpreted with some reservations. Although the independent security subtest of the avocational test is unsatisfactory in reliability, it does not seem to cut across the expected trends and may be included in the independent security total without loss of validity to the latter.

Mature Dependent Security

None of the inter-correlations between the mature dependent security subtests are as substantial as expected, but all are positive and statistically significant. The one that is most highly correlated with the mature dependent security total is the avocational subtest.

The mature dependent security subtest of the extra-familial test meets three of the four intra-test expectations satisfactorily, having a low negative correlation with the insecurity subtest, and positive correlations with the independent security and immature dependent security subtests. However, the correlation with the deputy agents subtest is a low negative instead of the expected zero, although this does not seem to be a serious departure from expectations. With respect to inter-test correlations most of the expectations are met. There are positive correlations with two of the three independent security subtests, with the independent security total, with two of the three immature dependent security subtests and with the immature dependent security total. There are zero correlations with three of the four deputy agents subtests and with the total. There are negative correlations with three of the four insecurity subtests and with the insecurity total. It must be concluded that the mature dependent security subtest of the extra-familial test is highly satisfactory in meeting the expectations derived from the rationale.

The mature dependent security subtest of the avocational test is much less satisfactory. In the intra-test correlations it meets expectations only in that there is a positive correlation with the independent security subtest of the avocational test. There is a low positive rather than a zero correlation with the deputy agents subtest, a zero rather than a positive correlation with the immature dependent security subtest, and a zero rather than a negative correlation with the insecurity subtest. The inter-test correlations also show some unexpected trends. The correlations with independent security are zero rather than positive as expected, the correlations with insecurity are zero rather than negative, the correlations with deputy agents are all significantly positive rather than zero, and there are positive correlations with all of the immature dependent security subtests and with the total. In short, this mature dependent security subtest fulfils all the expectations of an immature dependent security subtest, and hence seems to reflect too large a measure of immature dependent security to be a valid measure of mature dependent security. This was the defect in the equivalent subtest of the first version of the avocational test and the revision has not overcome the difficulty.

The mature dependent subtest of the philosophical test comes out considerably better. Both in the intra-test and inter-test relationships, the expected positive correlations with the immature dependent security subtests are found, and in the inter-test correlations the expected positive correlations with the independent security subtests emerge. None of these correlations are substantial, and this is also desirable. Unlike the other mature dependent security subtests, this one is not expected to be negatively related to insecurity, since the rationale implies tolerance for insecurity. On the whole, this expectation is met; there is a significant but low negative correlation with the insecurity subtest of the philosophical test, but the correlations with the other insecurity subtests and with the insecurity total are not significant. The zero correlations with the deputy agents subtests and total are consistent with expectations. It may be concluded that the present version of this subtest is satisfactory and a great improvement upon the earlier version which had too great a tendency to overlap both with independent security and with insecurity.

The mature dependent security total fits in with the expectations from the rationale less satisfactorily than the mature dependent security subtests of either the extra-familial or philosophical tests. In general, it seems too highly influenced by the mature dependent security subtest of the avocational test, which was considered to be invalid. There are positive correlations with the independent security and immature dependent security subtests as required by the rationale, but the positive correlations with the deputy agents subtests and the zero correlations with the insecurity subtests are out of line with requirements.

Immature Dependent Security

The first expectation to be fulfilled is that all the immature dependent security subtests should be positively correlated with each other. This is fulfilled in the case of the familial, extra-familial and philosophical subtests, although the correlations are less substantial than expected. But it is clear that whatever is being measured by the immature dependent security subtest of the avocational test it is not what the other immature dependent security subtests measure, since in every case the correlations approximate zero.

The immature dependent security subtest of the familial test meets expectations fairly well with respect to both intra-test and inter-test correlations. There are low positive correlations with the insecurity and deputy agents totals, although not with all of the component subtests. There is the expected low positive correlation with the mature dependent security total and with two of the three mature dependent security subtests. The correlations with independent security are as expected: negative with the independent security subtest of the familial test and zero with the other independent security subtests and with the total.

The immature dependent security subtest of the extra-familial test seems equally satisfactory, fulfilling all of the intra-test and inter-test expectations, except that the positive correlations with two of the four deputy agents subtests are too low to be significant, and there is a zero rather than a low positive correlation with one of the insecurity subtests. None of these exceptions to the expectations seems important enough to detract from the general picture of validity of this subtest.

Of the four immature dependent security subtests, the one in the avocational test was the least satisfactory in meeting the expectations from the rationale. It tends to be positively correlated with independent security, rather than uncorrelated as expected. It proves to be un-correlated with mature dependent security, deputy agents and in-security, rather than positively correlated as expected. It has no significant correlation with the other subtests measuring immature dependent security. This subtest was intended to reflect enjoyment of a passive and recipient role in leisure time activities. The inter-correlations indicate that such a role is by no means confined to persons whose security rests on immature dependence in other areas of adjustment, and it is not entirely incompatible even with independent security. Paradoxically, the mature dependent security subtest of the avocational test, with its emphasis upon participation with other people in the enjoyment of avocational pursuits, seems to fit in better with the expectations for an immature dependent security subtest than the immature dependent security subtest itself. It may be that an otherwise independent or mature dependent and secure person can afford to be passive and recipient in his avocations, perhaps because our culture so strongly encourages this orientation.

The immature dependent security subtest of the philosophical test meets the expectations of the rationale fairly satisfactorily. Both in the intra-test and inter-test comparisons there is the positive relationship expected with both mature dependent security and deputy agents subtests and total, and the zero correlation expected with the independent security subtests. The chief discrepancy from expectations is that the correlations of the insecurity subtests and total is zero rather than the expected low negative. There is no necessity to conclude that this invalidates the subtest. On the contrary, an immature dependent adjustment in the philosophical area serves as a better protection against insecurity than an immature dependent adjustment in other areas. This might well have been expected on the basis of the rationale.

The immature dependent security total is entirely satisfactory in meeting the expectations of the rationale. It is positively correlated with both insecurity and deputy agents, and these correlations tend to be low as expected, while the positive correlation with mature dependent security is a more substantial one. The correlations with the independent security total and two of the three independent security subtests is zero, as expected.

Deputy Agents

Next to the insecurity subtests, the deputy agents subtests are most satisfactory in meeting the expectation that like subtests in different tests will be correlated positively. The inter-correlations obtained are all positive and all statistically significant. About half of them are substantial in degree. The lowest correlations are found in the case of the familial subtest. It may be recalled that this subtest included a number of items that did not meet the criterion of internal consistency, and that the coefficient of reliability was unsatisfactory.

The deputy agents subtests are all satisfactory in meeting the chief requirements of the rationale, namely, that there should be positive correlations with the insecurity subtest. All of the obtained correlations are significant, and, except in the case of the deputy agents subtest of the familial test, the correlations tend to be fairly substantial rather than low.

In examining the degree to which the expectation of low positive inter-correlations between deputy agents and immature dependent security subtests is met, it is possible to leave out of consideration the immature dependent security subtest of the avocational test, since it has already been found to be at odds with expectations. When this is done, all the remaining inter-correlations are positive in sign, although some of them are so low as to fall below the 5 per cent level of significance. However, all of the deputy agents subtests have significant positive correlations with the immature dependent security total. The deputy agents subtest of the familial test seems most closely related to the immature dependent security subtests, as might be expected from the content of the items it contains.

The correlations of the deputy agents subtests with the independent security subtests are all zero, as expected, except for a positive correlation between the deputy agents subtest of the familial test and the independent security subtest of the avocational test; both of these subtests are also of unsatisfactory reliability. The expectations of zero correlations with the mature dependent security subtests are met fairly consistently, provided that the mature dependent security subtest of the avocational subtest is not considered, on the grounds that it seems to reflect immature dependent security. It seems likely that the mature dependent security total has been influenced by this subtest, since correlations between it and the deputy agents subtests are all significantly positive. The only slight departure from expectations apart from this subtest is the low but significant negative correlation between the deputy agents and mature dependent security subtests of the extra-familial test; this departure does not seem to be incompatible with the rationale even though it was not expected.

The deputy agents total is satisfactory in meeting expectations. There are moderate positive correlations with the insecurity subtests and a fairly substantial positive correlation with the insecurity total. There are the expected low positive correlations with the immature dependent security total and with all of its component subtests, except for the avocational subtest, which has been proven to be unsatisfactory. The correlations with the independent and mature dependent security subtests are all zero as expected, except for a positive correlation with the avocational subtest which is also thought to be an unsatisfactory subtest.

On the whole, the deputy agents subtests meet expectations very well indeed. The weakest subtest is that in the familial test, which, as reported in an earlier section, is of questionable reliability.

X CONCLUSIONS

The conclusions to be drawn from the findings reported here centre around two chief issues. First, are the tests as they stand reliable and valid enough to be put into practical use either separately or as a battery? Second, what aspects of these tests should be given special attention when further revisions are undertaken? These two issues are interrelated to some extent, for the subtests that prove to be least reliable and valid are obviously those most in need of revision. Nevertheless, we shall examine first the question of the advisability of using the tests as they stand.

Let us first consider whether the tests could be used separately. The chief factor here is reliability. All but two of the subtests meet the customary requirements for a subtest, on the understanding that the subtest scores will subsequently be combined together in some way to give a total measure. When like subtests in the total battery of four tests are combined in this way to give measures of independent security, mature dependent security, immature dependent security, deputy agents and insecurity they do indeed achieve a degree of reliability high enough that they might be used for screening purposes. The reliability of the subtests does not seem high enough for the tests to be used separately, since no way has been provided to combine the subtests of any one test together into a total score. For use as separate measures within any one area of adjustment the subtests in each of the four tests should be extended in length in order to increase reliability. This would be a profitable direction for future development.

Even though their separate use is not recommended at the present time, let us next consider the four tests separately. Of the four, the extra-familial test seems to be the most satisfactory. Only seven of its forty-two items failed to meet the criteria of percentage endorsement and internal consistency. The reliability of all subtests ranges from fairly good to good. The distributions of the scores within the independent and mature dependent security subtests approximate a normal distribution, although the distributions for the other subtests are somewhat skewed. All subtests have high correlations with the subtest totals to which they contribute, and the deputy agents and insecurity subtests in particular are substantially related to other subtests of like kind. The intra-test correlations are very satisfactory in meeting the expectations derived from the rationale, as are the inter-test correlations, except in instances where the other subtests contributing to the correlation were themselves considered invalid.

The philosophical test is perhaps next most satisfactory, despite the fact that eleven of its thirty-six items do not meet the criteria of internal consistency and percentage endorsement. The reliability of all four subtests is satisfactory. The distribution of scores in the mature dependent security subtest is fairly normal, but the other distributions are skewed and in the case of the immature dependent security subtest the skew is extreme. The deputy agents and insecurity subtests have high positive correlations with their respective totals and substantial correlations with like subtests. The mature and immature dependent security subtests are less satisfactory in this respect, although the correlation of the mature dependent security subtest with the mature dependent security total is high. However, the expectations derived from the rationale were modified in view of special considerations pertinent to the philosophical area, and the inter-correlations obtained are quite congruent with this modified rationale.

There must be some reservations about the familial test. Of its thirty-six items, eight failed to meet the criteria of percentage endorsement and internal consistency, most of these being items of the deputy agents subtest. The low reliability of the latter subtest makes it of questionable usefulness, at least until such a time as another reliability check can be made with a Canadian population, this being one of the two subtests believed to be affected by cultural differences between Canadian and English populations. However, the deputy agent subtest, as well as the insecurity and immature dependent security subtests meet the validity criterion of congruency of inter-correlations with expectations derived from the rationale. This is a further reason for suggesting that the test is of questionable usefulness rather than distinctly unsatisfactory. The independent security subtest seems to be satisfactory, provided that when interpreting individual scores it is recalled that the emphasis is somewhat more upon the independent or emancipated aspect of independent security than upon the secure aspect.

The avocational test is the least satisfactory of the four tests. Intra-test and inter-test correlations suggest that neither the mature dependent security nor the immature dependent security subtest is congruent with expectations from the rationale, and hence they should be excluded from consideration if the test is used in a battery in its present form. Moreover, the independent security subtest contains items too frequently endorsed to yield coefficients of correlation high enough for either reliability or validity, although its intra-test and inter-test correlations are in the expected directions. To be sure, it was suggested that this subtest might prove satisfactory with a Canadian population despite the fact that it had been insufficiently discriminating with an English population. But if it is to be included in a battery it should be used with great caution until such time as it is proved satisfactory with the population in question. Both the insecurity and the deputy agents subtests seem to meet the criteria of reliability and validity reasonably well and therefore might be included in a test battery.

If the four tests are to be used in a battery there are two ways in which the subtest scores may be handled. One way is to consider the eighteen subtest scores separately, ignoring the mature and immature dependent security subtest scores of the avocational test as being invalid, and using the deputy agents score for the familial test and the independent security score for the avocational test with considerable reservation. This type of analysis could be used to yield a profile indicating the chief areas of strength and weakness. The relatively low reliabilities of the separate subtests would require that only extremely high or extremely low points on the profile be considered significant. This method of handling the subtest scores should be used only as a supplement to the second, more satisfactory method.

The second method of handling the subtest scores is to combine them into total scores. The reliability coefficients for the totals were found to be much higher on the whole than the reliability coefficients of the component subtests. Moreover, the inter-correlations suggest that four of the five total scores have as high or higher validity than any of the component subtests. The exception is the mature dependent security total, which seems to be too greatly influenced by the invalid avocational subtest. It would seem desirable to omit this subtest and use only the mature dependent security subtests of the extra-familial and philosophical tests, either separately or combined. The immature dependent security subtest of the avocational test does not seem to have the same undesirable effect on the immature dependent security total, but it would probably prove to be more satisfactory to exclude it from the immature dependent security total. In summary, it is recommended that the following scores be obtained for the battery:

(*a*) An independent security score, obtained by totalling the scores of the independent security subtests of the familial, extra-familial and avocational tests.

(*b*) A mature dependent security score, obtained by totalling the scores of the mature dependent security subtests of the extra-familial and philosophical tests.

(*c*) An immature dependent security score, obtained by totalling the scores of the immature dependent security subtests of the familial, extra-familial and philosophical subtests.

(*d*) An insecurity score obtained by totalling the scores of the insecurity subtests of all four tests.

(*e*) A deputy agents score obtained by totalling the scores of the deputy agents subtests of all four tests.

It cannot be assumed that the exclusion of unsatisfactory items from tests or the exclusion of unsatisfactory tests or subtests from a battery will leave the statistical findings to be obtained from the remaining items, subtests, or tests the same. However, it is expected that the changes would be in the direction of an improvement in both reliability and validity, although this cannot be taken as a certainty. Nevertheless, we recommend that if the tests are to be put to practical use without further revision, the unsatisfactory items should be dropped (except those items which have been pointed out as having been satisfactory with Canadian populations) and either the avocational test as a whole should be excluded from the battery, or the independent security, deputy agents and insecurity subtests should be retained and the mature and immature dependent security subtests be dropped.

The above recommendation could not be made if norms had been established for the present tests and presented for use. Since normative research has not yet been undertaken, it would be impossible in any case to appraise an individual without reference to the particular group of which he is a member. It is therefore suggested that the tests are ready for use for screening purposes only in situations in which the group to be tested is large enough to provide its own norms.

A word of caution must be added. Tests of this sort require co-operation and frankness of the subjects. If the tests were presented as being crucially important in a screening or selection situation in which many individuals were highly motivated either towards or against selection, it can be confidently predicted that much would be lost with respect both to reliability and to validity. On the other hand, if the tests can be presented either as potentially helpful to the individual or as part of routine information that is being collected, it is believed that this battery is of considerable potential usefulness in screening, either for selection or for the detection of individuals in the group who should be appraised more thoroughly and possibly given counselling or therapy. The test battery should be especially effective in identifying individuals with a high degree of manifest insecurity and those who are unduly defensive. An unusually large number of "cannot say" answers, as well as a high score on the deputy agents total, would point to the over-defensive individual as suggested by Cronbach (4).

Although it is believed that this battery has now been refined sufficiently to be useful practically as specified above, it is obvious that further revision is desirable. Items that proved to be unsatisfactory either because of too high or too low frequency of endorsement or because of low consistency with the subtest in question should be replaced by others. Skewed distributions might be improved by revision of infrequently (or too frequently) endorsed items, and this should also increase reliability. And, if the tests are to be used separately rather than in a battery, all subtests should be enlarged, using the present satisfactory items as a nucleus for the revision.

This type of refinement seems to be all that is required for the extra-familial and philosophical tests. Further revision of the familial test is desirable with particular attention to the independent security and deputy agents subtests. The independent security subtest still does not reflect *security* to the desired extent and is still too much concerned with emancipation from family ties. There is no clear-cut line for revision of the deputy agents subtest, so exploration would be required. In the avocational test three subtests need revision. The independent security subtest seems to be satisfactory except for too frequent endorsement of the items, and this may rectify itself when the test is tried again with other populations. However, the mature and immature dependent security subtests need complete revision, and it is quite likely that the rationale of these two subtests should be reconsidered.

The discussion of further research cannot be concluded without mention of the desirability of normative studies and further validation research. The former are needed so obviously as to require no further discussion, but there are aspects of the latter that deserve mention.

The criterion of validity employed in this study was considered an essential first criterion. A very similar and possibly more effective use of this criterion could be accomplished through factor analysis. This had been considered in the present study, but since so many of the subtests represented a radical departure from equivalent subtests in earlier revisions, it was not thought desirable to introduce factor analysis until it had been determined that all the component measures yielded inter-correlations congruent with the rationale.

This does not imply that an examination of internal relationships within the battery is believed to be the final approach to validation, or that it can take the place of validation of the component subtests against appropriate outside criteria. But formidable difficulties arise when one attempts to select appropriate outside criteria against which to validate measures that are defined in terms of the subjective experience of the individual. There is probably no single criterion that could serve for a conclusive demonstration of validity of any of the component subtests. Probably, the best that could be done would be to select a variety of criteria, correlation with which would offer indirect evidence of validity of the measures in question. In the meantime, it is believed that the validation by congruency that has been undertaken in this study is not insignificant. It is likely that this is the best criterion of validity possible in the case of measures of subjective experience, and that the desirable additional validation research could be considered as a supplement rather than as a substitute. It is believed that the most essential step towards validation is to repeat the same study with a new population in order to check the reliability if the inter-correlations upon which the present case for validity rests.

BIBLIOGRAPHY

1. AINSWORTH, L. H. "Rigidity as a Manifestation of Insecurity." Unpublished M.A. thesis, University of Toronto, 1950.
2. AINSWORTH, L. H. "Rigidity, Insecurity and Stress." *Journal of Abnormal and Social Psychology*, 56 (1958), 67–74.
3. BLUM, M. H. "Security of Adolescents in the Use of Money." Studies in Security, no. 10. Unpublished M.A. thesis, University of Toronto, 1950.
4. CRONBACH, J. L. "Further Evidence on Response Sets and Test Design," *Educational and Psychological Measurement*, 6 (1946), 475–94.
5. FERGUSON, G. A. *The Reliability of Mental Tests.* London: University of London Press, 1941.
6. GRAPKO, M. F. "The Relation of Certain Psychological Variables to Security: A Contribution to Theory." Unpublished Ph.D. thesis, University of Toronto, 1953.
7. HOYT, C. "Test Reliability Obtained by Analysis of Variance," *Psychometrika*, 6 (1941), 153–60.
8. LAIDLAW, R. G. N. "Security in the Academic Area." Unpublished M.A. thesis, University of Toronto, 1949.
9. LAURENCE, M. "A Clarification of the Concept in the Familial Area." Studies in the Concept of Security, no. 1. Unpublished M.A. thesis, University of Toronto, 1949.
10. SALTER, M. D. "The Concept of Security as a Basis for the Evaluation of Adjustment." Unpublished Ph.D. thesis, University of Toronto, 1939.
11. SALTER, M. D. *An Evaluation of Adjustment Based upon the Concept of Security.* University of Toronto Studies, Child Development Series, no. 18, 1940.
12. TOBIN, S. M. "A Clarification of the Concept of Security in the Vocational Area." Unpublished M.A. thesis, University of Toronto, 1950.
13. WALTER, O. J. "A Clarification of the Concept of Security in the Area of Competition." Unpublished M.A. thesis, University of Toronto, 1950.
14. WHITEHOUSE, D. W. "Belongingness: Its Nature and Measurement." Studies in Security, no. 8. Unpublished M.A. thesis, University of Toronto, 1950.

APPENDIX

FAMILIAL TEST

(Third Revision)

Independent Security

1. Although I value the affection my parents hold for me, I feel that I do not need it to make me feel confident in myself.
2. I feel on very good terms with my parents, despite the fact that I no longer rely on them for help or advice.
6. I enjoy the comfortable feeling that I can handle any problem that might come my way without help from my parents.
15. Although I get on very well with my parents, I do not feel that loss or separation would make any great difference to my life in general.
20. I feel comfortably free to make my own arrangements with my friends without talking it over with my parents.
36. One of the reasons that I get along so well with my parents is that I never feel held in by their disapproval.

Immature Dependent Security

3. I feel so close to my parents that I feel that they will always be my closest friends.
7. I feel very much at home with my parents, more so than with anyone else that I have ever met.
16. It is a great comfort to me to realize that I can always count on my parents to help me out of a jam.
19. It is a great comfort to me that my parents help me to make up my mind.
25. It is a great comfort to have my parents help me such a lot.
26. I am happy to fall back on my parents to do the many little things for me that tend to make life more comfortable.

Insecurity

4. The nagging I get from my parents sometimes irritates me very much.
8. I am concerned that my relationship with my parents is not all that it might be.
11. I often feel very regretful that I have not fulfilled my obligations to my parents.
12. When the going gets tough I often wish that I were back in the happy days of my childhood.
17. I often get a troubled feeling from wondering if my parents might disapprove of what I am doing.
18. My family are very kind to me, but I am sorry that I do not have a real warm relationship with them.

23. I feel discouraged that it is so difficult to live up to what my parents expect of me.
24. It makes me feel uneasy to think of being completely on my own.
27. I often feel a sense of regret that I have not had as happy a family life as other people have had.
30. It bothers me that my parents do not allow me to be more on my own.
31. It discourages me that my parents interfere so much in my life.
32. I sometimes worry about the future as a time when I will not get as much help from my parents as I do now.

Deputy Agents

5. I feel a little natural resentment towards anyone in a position to tell me what to do.
9. I am apt to do things so thoroughly that I can't possibly do all the other things I should be doing.
10. Although I don't get on very well with my parents, I don't let this bother me, and try to live my own life.
13. I always tend to put off making a decision until the very last minute.
14. I find it difficult to get things done in time.
21. It makes me feel very uncomfortable if pressure of time forces me to leave some things done poorly or incompletely.
22. It makes me feel uncomfortable if something prevents me from having things neat and tidy.
28. I know my parents worry about the things I do, but I don't let this bother me, and try to live my own life.
29. One of the most important factors in helping me decide on something is whether or not it will please my parents.
33. I would feel guilty if I felt that I were letting my parents down in any way.
34. I would feel very hesitant to embark on a course of action which my parents might consider wrong.
35. I feel sure that I can never do better than live up to the values that my parents hold.

EXTRA-FAMILIAL TEST

(Second Revision)

Independent Security

2. I feel quite confident of myself when I am with other people.
8. I feel quite comfortable about how I stand in the eyes of the people I am usually with.
17. I gain satisfaction from being able to do things well, and this feeling is not lessened when I find other people can do things better.
24. I don't think about it much, but I feel able to hold my own in any group.

34. I do enough things well that I feel quite assured of myself in any group of people that I might be with.
36. Status and prestige do not matter to me because I feel I have my own share.

Mature Dependent Security

1. I feel so much at home with people that it never occurs to me to feel left out of things.
9. I get so much satisfaction from my intimate friendships, that it hardly ever occurs to me to be concerned about whether or not people like me.
16. There is at least one group of people outside my family with whom I feel really at home, and in whose activities I can really join.
25. I often have a really warm feeling of "being in tune with" my friends.
35. I never feel uneasy with my friends for fear I'm not getting on with them.
39. I get a great deal of pleasure from having at least one intimate friend whom I can trust and who trusts me.

Immature Dependent Security

3. I am very glad that my friends approve of me, for I am very sensitive to disapproval.
4. I try very hard to make people like me, and I am satisfied that I nearly always succeed.
10. It is a comfort to me that I can count on my friends to help in making decisions.
18. It is a comfort to me that my friends give me so much help and support.
19. I have friends whose help gives me the confidence in myself that I need.
26. It gives me comfort to know that I have one or two good friends upon whom I can lean for help and encouragement.

Insecurity

5. I sometimes feel left out of things.
11. I feel uncomfortable about how I stand in the eyes of the people I am usually with.
12. I sometimes feel sad, for there is no one to whom I feel really close.
22. Sometimes I feel unhappy because no one really understands me.
23. When I am unhappy, I wish I had someone in whom I could confide.
27. I am very uncomfortable when I feel that I am disapproved of.
28. I am easily embarrassed in social situations.
37. Sometimes I have an unhappy feeling that people do not like me.
38. Sometimes when I am with people I have feeling that I do not "fit in."
40. It makes me feel very uncomfortable to feel that someone dislikes me.
41. I am sometimes disappointed in my friends because they let me down when I need them.
42. I feel handicapped by my lack of self-confidence when I am with people.

Deputy Agents

6. I think the best way to get along socially is to be able to do a lot of things well.
7. I don't worry about feeling left out, because I know I can learn to do things that will make people respect me.
13. I enjoy being with intelligent, popular people because I feel more important myself when I am with them.
14. I have a lot of friends but don't feel really close to any of them.
15. I may hurt people by the things I do, but I feel that this cannot be helped if you want to live your own life.
20. I am inclined to view strangers as intruders.
21. I like my friends to be of at least my own social standing.
29. It makes me uncomfortable not to know clearly what is expected of me.
30. It makes me feel uneasy to feel different from my friends.
31. Other people often irritate me.
32. I feel at my best in organized group activity.
33. I do not want to feel very near and dear to anyone.

AVOCATIONAL TEST

(First Revision)

Independent Security

2. I really look forward to my spare time, even when alone, because there are so many interesting things to do.
11. In my spare time I like to spend hours at a stretch doing something that interests me.
16. I don't need to depend on other people to keep me from being bored in my spare time, for there are lots of things that I enjoy doing by myself.
17. I am confident that I can fully occupy my spare time with my varied interests.
24. I enjoy learning new things and developing new interests in my spare time.
29. I enjoy doing something creative in my spare time.

Mature Dependent Security

1. I look forward to my spare time as an opportunity to participate with other people in the games or sports that I like.
12. I find special pleasure in developing spare-time skills with friends.
18. I have many spare time interests which I enjoy with my friends.
19. I enjoy spending my spare time with my friends learning new things together.

34. I enjoy improving my skill in the spare-time things I do with other people.
39. I am glad that I can spend my spare time with other people, for I very much enjoy the feeling of team work that group activity gives me.

Immature Dependent Security

3. I enjoy spending my spare time going to the movies, or watching games, or listening to the radio.
13. I like to relax in my spare time, and let other people do the entertaining.
15. I enjoy my spare time, especially when no effort is required of me.
25. I find it quite satisfying to pass time watching games or other forms of entertainment without wanting to take part in them myself.
26. I enjoy being with other people in my spare time even though I don't contribute much to group activity.
30. I enjoy just relaxing and doing nothing in my spare time.

Insecurity

4. I often find myself bored during my spare time, and don't seem to be able to find anything interesting to do.
5. There are times when I feel bored and restless, and do not seem to be able to enter into anything with real enjoyment.
9. Although I manage to keep my spare time fully occupied, I sometimes regret that I don't enjoy myself more.
10. Although I ordinarily enjoy myself in my spare time, sometimes things seem to turn sour, and I feel unhappy without something to absorb my attention.
14. I sometimes waste my spare time without especially enjoying myself.
22. I like to plan ahead for my spare time, and am bored when I have been unable to arrange anything special to do.
23. It disturbs me that I can't find interesting things to do in my spare time.
31. I sometimes think my life is dull and uninteresting.
35. I am inclined to feel restless in my spare time.
36. Sometimes I feel too tense to be able to relax in my spare time.
40. It bothers me that I can't settle down to any one thing in my spare time.

Deputy Agents

6. I enjoy my spare time so much that I neglect my work and responsibilities.
7. I like to spend my spare time in worthwhile activities and feel I have wasted it if I just spend it pleasantly doing nothing of particular value.
8. When I have nothing in particular to do, I find myself wishing that something exciting would happen.
20. I like to spend my spare time developing skills that will help me win the admiration and respect of other people.
21. I feel that the best use to which I can put my spare time is in learning things that will help me get ahead.

27. I personally like a little excitement in my spare time, and think the way lots of people amuse themselves is pretty dull.
28. I like to keep busy all the time, otherwise I get bored.
32. I am so busy with my work and other things that I have hardly any spare time.
33. I fill up my spare time with so many responsible activities that it is really more like work than play.
37. I tend to be bored at a party without a few drinks.
38. I would like to start some skilled spare time work but I haven't the time.
41. All the things that I would like to do cost more than I can afford.

PHILOSOPHICAL TEST

(First Revision)

Mature Dependent Security

1. I have worked out a philosophy for living that gives me confidence that I can meet any crises that life may bring.
6. It makes me happy to feel that I have a worthwhile place in the world.
11. I feel I am becoming more and more the kind of person I want to be.
16. I feel a pleasant sense of achievement in knowing that my philosophy of life is based, on the whole, on my own personal grappling with problems.
17. I feel a sense of ease in knowing what I want from life is good and is generally within my reach.
36. I feel a sense of purpose in life and can therefore accept the fact that I shall never know the final truths about life and death.

Immature Dependent Security

3. I have peace of mind because I know that my best interests will always be looked after by a higher power.
10. I fully accept our society's ideas about what is right and wrong.
15. My religion is good because it has definite rules that I can follow.
21. I'm happy to have a philosophy that I need not understand.
23. I feel easy in my mind when doubt arises because there is always someone I can consult for the answers.
27. It gives me peace of mind to know that my fate is decided beforehand.

Insecurity

2. I feel upset because I can't make my life what I want it to be.
5. I cannot really accept the religious beliefs in which I was brought up, yet at times I feel guilty about not being able to.
7. I feel helpless because there are so many things that I am unable to control.

13. I often feel critical of myself for not living up to what I should be.
14. At times I feel a real concern that my ideas about life are getting farther and farther away from those held by my parents.
18. I feel uneasy about what lies in store for me in life.
19. I deeply regret knowing that I can never undo all my wrongdoings.
24. I am despondent about the cruelty of mankind.
28. I feel uneasy when I consider life, death and the hereafter.
29. I sometimes feel that I am useless and unworthy.
31. I feel that my life is without purpose.
34. I feel uneasy because I have no future aims that seem worthwhile.

Deputy Agents

4. There is so little that one person can do about the world that it is useless to waste time thinking about it.
8. "Just take what comes and let tomorrow look after itself" is my motto.
9. I feel a certain relief in thinking that my present personal behaviour will not matter a hundred years from now.
12. I have no worries about breaking the moral code, because I have learned that all morals are relative anyhow.
20. It helps me to believe in a person who can make me forget my own worries.
22. I admit I feel intolerant of other people's beliefs when I know they are wrong.
25. Any moral code is wrong that inhibits man's natural needs.
26. I don't believe it is any good worrying about good and bad, for there is nothing one can do about it anyway.
30. I think that people who are tolerant are only fooling themselves.
32. I can't help but feel impatient that other people are so stubborn in refusing to accept the truth.
33. It makes me feel good to belong to a strong and worthwhile organization much bigger and more important than myself.
35. Since there is so little I can do to control things, I figure that I might just as well have a good time and forget about the future.

INDEX